Copyright 2023, Pierre-Louis Ours

THE ROCK BREAKS THE GLOBALISTS EMPIRE

First edition. July 16, 2023.

Copyright © 2023 Pierre-Louis Ours.

ISBN: 979-8224875542

Written by Pierre-Louis Ours.

Table of Contents

The Rock Breaks

the [Globalists'] Empire

Remember Whose Universe This Is...

Preface

Crooked leaders cannot be your friends.

They use the law to cause suffering.

They join forces against people who do right

and sentence to death the innocent.

But the Lord is my defender;

my God is the rock of my protection.

God will pay them back for their sins

and will destroy them for their evil.

The Lord our God will destroy them.

Psalm 94:20 – 23 NCV

Table of contents

Introduction

When the follower of Jesus considers the state of the world we live in, he seeks to know where we are in the scale of time in order to understand why things are what they are. It is also a natural reflex to peer into what may be coming. One can try to read the tea leaves or one can search what prophecies have yet to actualize and under what conditions.

As I pondered this a few years ago, one event stuck out in particular: the second and complete exodus of the Hebrew people into the land of Israel. It is the most documented event in the Jewish and Christian scriptures—save Messiah. It struck me that according to prophecy this exodus 2.0 will follow a similar script as Moses' in antiquity; the prophecies are clear about this. And this is the point that is relevant to us all today.

Exodus 1.0 was opposed by the Egyptian powers of the state. Pharaoh and his administration did not want to lose their slavish workforce or lose face in the eyes of the nations surrounding Egypt. Pharaoh and Egypt were destroyed in the process.

But Pharaoh and his government were only the useful idiots of the power behind the scene: Satan. Indeed, Satan knew the stakes: the whole region would see the power of the true God when He destroyed Egypt. They would see the God of the Hebrews divinely lead His people out and provide for them in the desert. They would see God bring them unerringly to the land He had promised them. And there, the whole world would see God's interaction with people. The world population would get the scriptures. The Savior of the world would come to Israel, through Israel as promised and He would atone for the ills of the world. From Israel, the Good News would propagate and this new alliance would change the world, having wrenched the vise-like power of Satan. This is what was at stake.

What is at stake with exodus 2.0? This: The whole world—on telephone screens, tablets, TV...—will see the only true God revealed in action. The Hebrews who accept the new alliance will all embrace Messiah and wildly celebrate in the land of Israel. Everyone in the world will know this and study it. God will rejoice and celebrate.

Exodus 2.0 will induce the world to ask questions about the God they have seen. A cosmic change will have happened through a series of events that will have altered the world's routine and the expectations of people everywhere. This is what is at stake this time.

Exodus 2.0 is universal; it is not limited to any country in particular like exodus 1.0 was: Today, the Hebrews are scattered everywhere. Satan must desperately oppose this and try to prevent it. We are experiencing this all-out effort to derail God's awesome plan. This is why things are so crazy now across the globe and getting crazier.

Who are the modern useful idiots in the service of Satan who will blindly oppose this exodus on the human level? Just like in Egypt, when Pharaoh could not "afford" to let exodus 1.0 happen; a new world power, Satanistic in nature, must oppose this divine intervention or their entire aim at world control falls apart. This power is the very destructive Globalist One-World-Government/New-World-Order. This unelected, elite "empire" destroys all individualities: it eliminates borders, nationalities, sexes, religions, etc. It aims at creating a class of nondescript humanity held in the bondage of slavery to a tiny world elite. So, for them, when one well-defined ethnic group (Hebrews) escapes their control and begin to live as a "people apart" and worse yet, if this group worships and magnifies the Creator; the entire premise of One-World-Government/New-World-Order is dead. So exodus 2.0 is an existential threat to them.

Conversely, the complete exodus 2.0 of the French Hebrews does not bother the average French person. The same is true for the Italian Hebrews and the same applies to every country. Exodus 2.0 will be applauded in the United States of America by all the true Christians. So, the opposer to exodus 2.0 will be distinct from most autochthon populations.

The process of exodus 2.0 is clear and easy to follow. Just as Pharaoh's power structure was destroyed by God prior to exodus 1.0; we can expect the absolute destruction of the Globalists empire and its elite before exodus 2.0 takes place. How, when and in what context is the content of this essay.

The end of the Globalists' New-World-Order is not a stand-alone event. It is an intrinsic part of a series of predicted events; it is thus impossible to address the subject outside its greater context. Therefore, dealing with the end of the Globalists' New-World-Order, this essay, by necessity and for clarity, must give an overview of the other events and their foretold process. I will go back and forth between the different events to move all the threads along; so bear with me.

Do we live in a world gone mad or are we witnesses to a majestically orchestrated plan? It is easy to see the world-gone-mad part; but the followers of Jesus have the information to watch the divinely orchestrated plan coming to fruition. Let us form the effective mental picture that the Bible gives us. This is the subject of this exposé.

I am not writing a prophetic piece, I have no ambition that way. Also, I am not connected to the "Powers-that-be" machine. I do not have access to the "right people," and I do not have a personal agenda in any of this. Also, I do not have special, privileged knowledge; I am simply a witness—a spectator; a watchman. I see what is happening and I search scriptures in order to *understand what will happen in the last days* (Peter

3:3). This is the presentation of what I see in the scriptures, a trigger to cause us to ponder. Read, pray, and may God lead you.

As with every individual human project, all the separate, developing components eventually converge to fill their specific, coordinated role in the completed whole. It is the same with humanity and with God's plan for humanity and for the world. We are at the time when the major threads of history and the remaining aspects of prophecy all converge. True followers of Jesus cannot continue to live, preach and hope as they have been for centuries.

Circumstances forced upon us have focused our eyes on the rock-strewn path of our modern world. It is hard to navigate safely the intricate pathway of the fast-paced life today; reflexively, we are busy looking down. We need to pause and look up, scan the scenery and the horizon and refocus on the goal of our journey. We live in the fourth empire revealed by God through Daniel. This empire is destructive, abusive, oppressive and hopeless. It is invasive at all levels and in all aspects of life. Living in this fourth empire keeps our eyes on the ground and hampers our Divine outlook. Yet, its fate is certain.

Understanding the process will situate the follower of Jesus in the right frames of mind, of history and of purpose. An alternate biblical title for this piece could be: Are we there yet? Because, indeed it is one of the vital questions. When I want to find my way through a mall, the basic information that will makes sense of the map is the stylized arrow that says: You are here. Without it, I would meander aimlessly and waste time and energy. This exposé finds the arrow.

The role of each converging line of prophecy is to reveal God to the world in a powerful and concrete manner. I call the series of events we will shortly encounter "God's march of glory". These events begin with the destruction of the Fourth Empire and culminate with the rapture of the saints.

Our situation

Are we there yet?

Let us enter into our modern reality.

Paul explicitly foretells us: *Remember this! In the last days there will be many troubles, because*

- *people will love themselves,*

- *love money,*

- *brag,*

- *and be proud.*

Can you relate?

- *They will say evil things against others*

- *and will not obey their parents*

- *or be thankful*

- *or be the kind of people God wants.*

- *They will not love others,*

- *will refuse to forgive,*

- *will gossip,*

- *and will not control themselves.*

- *They will be cruel,*

- *will hate what is good,*

- *will turn against their friends,*

- *and will do foolish things without thinking.*

- *They will be conceited,*

- *will love pleasure instead of God...* (2 Timothy 3:1 – 4 NCV Bullet points added).

Peter succinctly tells us: *It is most important for you to understand what will happen in the last days.*

- *People will laugh at you.*

- *They will be doing the evil things they want to do.* (2 Peter 3:3 NCV).

Peter does not tell us that it is OK to bury our heads in the sand and plod on unaware. It is "most important" that we should pay attention.

This is also the time when *"knowledge will increase"* (Daniel 12:4). As proposed above: knowledge of evil has indeed increased. Evil is trumpeted loud and clear at every street corner and rebroadcast ad nauseam for all to see.

Anyone with internet can instantly access archives, libraries and references and within seconds gain the available knowledge they seek. Knowledge in all categories is accessible like never before.

However, the reality we overlook is that knowledge has most importantly increased in the "good"—the knowledge of God's kingdom in God's kingdom. In the past, pockets of people had access to the knowledge of Messiah Jesus (traditional "Christian" lands and the lands where missionaries had gone and where the Word was translated into the local languages); but today, the knowledge and awareness of Messiah Jesus' reality is universally available (the internet is universal, and computerized translators are instantly available in all languages). Unlike before, everyone is now aware of "Jesus" in some ways. Everyone has access to the tools to research Him. Knowledge of Jesus has increased exponentially. Which means that the responsibility of our individual response to the knowledge of Messiah Jesus is now universal: we are all either personally guilty or have escaped our guilt. We have reached the time Jesus alludes to: *And the Good News I have shared about God's kingdom will be told throughout the world. It will be spread to every nation. Then the end will come* (Matthew 24:14 ERV). So, we are at the fulcrum of history when "the end will come" (or: when the events of the end will take place).

> <u>Note</u>: Jesus did not say that everybody in the world would become a believer; but that the Good News would be available—told or read. Nor did He say that everyone alive then would be involved in a bible study group. But He said that the Good News He shared will be made available to all nations throughout the world. And this has indeed happened. Technology has made it so. His words have happened.

This reality had never been the case universally since Noah. The implications of this reality are transformational.

So we have an increase in knowledge—of the good and of the evil. And we have a nefarious blooming of evil. Every evil listed above has existed through history; but these evils were not the norm, except in the era leading to the great flood of Noah's time. Today, not only these evils are the norm; they are forced upon those who morally resist. The epoch of

Noah is a harbinger, a precedent for us: God acted then; and thus God will act now.

On the other hand, we also have the most abundant blooming of righteous harvest ever. Indeed: Consider that in China there are now more than one hundred million true believers/followers of Jesus (this has never been so); in Iran, one million; and among the 270+ million people of officially Moslem Indonesia, 15% have converted to the Good News of Jesus; in Africa, tens of millions have... In America, the believers are being refined; the chaff is being exposed and cleared out. The righteous harvest is proceeding strongly, irreversibly.

Christianity has never contained as many living souls as today! The pundits who aver that we live in a post-Christian era are fools. Actually, worse than that: they acknowledge that there "was" Christianity—a faith based on Jesus' teachings—but they chose not to abide by it or abide in it; so they "went beyond". But one does not go beyond or post-Christianity: Christianity carry within itself a destination and a sure destiny. It does not stop short of its own destination. And it does not miss its destiny. In saying: "post-Christianity", these people disclaim to everyone that they have made their eternal choice: They have gone back to Adam's curse.

God had visited this subject and its times when He inspired Isaiah (as you read Isaiah 59, keep in mind that, unlike in Isaiah's time, Jesus is now known among the Gentiles. He is ubiquitous. Everyone in our societies knows of Him; so the following confession is appropriate): *We have done many wrong things against our God; our sins show we are wrong*, is something that every follower of Jesus—and everyone in our western societies—can confess to today. Isaiah's verses read: *We know we have turned against God; we know the evil things we have done:*

* *Sinning and rejecting the LORD,*

- *Turning away from our God,*

- *Planning to hurt others and disobey God,*

- *Planning and speaking lies.*

- *So we have driven away justice,*

- *And we have kept away from what is right.*

- *Truth is not spoken in the streets;*

- *What is honest is not allowed to enter the city.*

- *Truth cannot be found anywhere,*

- *And people who refuse to do evil are attacked.* (Bullets added)

Take the time to consider every bullet point above; each and every one of them defines our times, our society and our nation. And the pundits alluded to above can declare that we live in a post-Christian era precisely because they have turned against the God they <u>know</u> exists... and thus they do know the evil they have done. By saying: "post-Christian", they self-convict. Extrapolating from this: Can we see the similarities of our time with the times of Noah? Are we there yet? Yes, we are. So: God will act. Isaiah's text continues:

The LORD looked and could not find any justice, and He was displeased. He could not find anyone to help the people, and He was surprised that there was no one to help. **So He used His own power to save the people;** *His own goodness gave him strength. He covered Himself with goodness like armor. He put the helmet of salvation on His head. He put on the clothes of punishment and wrapped Himself in the coat of His strong love. The LORD will pay back His enemies for what they have done. He will show His anger to those who were against Him; He will punish the* *people in faraway places as they deserve.* (Emphasis added.) This does not require any interpretation; it is clear as given.

And why does God do all this? He tells us through Isaiah: *Then people from the west will fear the LORD, and people from the east will fear His glory.* This is The Great Revealing (emphasis is mine). As we will see, the purpose of every component of the "God's march of glory" is to graphically reveal God/Jesus to every living human.

The coming process has never happened in such a way in history. Indeed: God visibly leading His people out of Egypt with the pillars of cloud or of fire was a "localized" event. But today, the series of coming events will be universal events. The divine process will usher a completely new style of life. Everyone will have seen God in action. Nothing will be the same. The ultimate purpose of the process is the great harvest of souls, as we will develop in the text.

How will God do this? *The LORD will come quickly like a fast flowing river, driven by the breath of the LORD.* And, each of the cataclysmic interventions will be seen and felt by everyone, everywhere.

Then, God places Isaiah's prophecy in its historical context: *Then a Savior will come to Jerusalem and to the people of Jacob who have turned from sin, says the LORD.* One of the steps of "God's march of Glory" is the return of the righteous Hebrews to the land of Israel where they will all get to know their savior Jesus, the One they had spurned. This verse does not refer to the first coming of Jesus because the people of Jacob, in the whole, did not turn from sin then. This does not allude to the time when Jesus will return to reign on earth, because at that time, He will reign on all remaining people (that is all the righteous people of Jacob that God kept safe in their desert haven <u>and</u> all the Hell bound, marked Gentiles who survived the "time of testing").

It all fits: *...a Savior will come to Jerusalem and to the people of Jacob who have turned from sin, says the LORD*. It refers to the seven+ years of Jesus' rejoicing in Israel, the years that follow Gog and Magog and precede the rapture of the believers—a period within our own era (see Ezekiel 38 – 39).

The rising fears of the good People

"Oh my gosh! This is the age of the antichrist!..." I read this types of comments, I hear them being retold often.

How do you feel about some of the following: The impending great reset of the One-World-Government/New-World-Order? The implementation of the universal surveillance state, by the "bad guys" but also by the "good guys"? The branding or chipping or chemical marking of the populations? The systematic suppression of truth? The centrally controlled genetic manipulations? The systematic cretinization of the masses? The mind-reading and mind-altering controls? Aren't these the apparatus of the antichrist being set up? Are we seeing the antichrist rule being installed?

Nope, we are not—everything has its place and purpose.

Christians, usually in a panic, broadcast their perceptions of the signs of the antichrist, of 666. We hear and read all sorts of cooky theories and mis-adaptations of scriptures imaginable. Preachers and writers turn Daniel 9 completely on its head and insert the antichrist in it. We hear all kinds of extra-biblical tidbits about how we are seeing the four horses of the Apocalypse and many other inane nonsense. By the way: Have you noticed that these considerations do not bother the non-believers at all? ... But they emotionally distress those who follow Jesus—those who ought to know better.

We are being played. Shame on us. This is not a time to be a casual believer. We must know and understand what we believe.

When I shut the door on the outside clamor and paranoia and sift through these issues with the scriptures in mind I noticed the following principles. Read on and make up your own judgment.

The AntiChrist

To begin with: The antichrist is no factor today—even though forms of his persona are manifest; as they have throughout history. The text of Revelation is clear that Satan identifies and empowers the antichrist <u>after</u> the Hebrews are <u>all</u> moved effortlessly and safely out of the land of Israel and into their desert enclave and furthermore: this all happen <u>after</u> Satan and the demons are thrown down out of heaven. These markers are not negotiable; and none of these markers have been effected today. The complete Hebrew population (the two southern kingdom tribes and the 10 northern kingdom tribes) has yet to be returned to the land of Israel as a comprehensive group (exodus 2.0); let alone been all moved to a desert haven. (We will cover the State of Israel later in the text.)

Ah, but some will say: this is only the preparation so that all will be ready for the antichrist's complete control over people. It is not so. The antichrist will rule only because Jesus will make it possible. Jesus describes the short rule of the actual antichrist as the "time of testing" (Revelation 3:10). A time of assaying the hearts and souls, a time when every Gentile left on this earth will be sorted out. The conditions of life on the planet will be very different then; but humans will still be fully human. They will not be cyborgs, they will not be chemically altered mutants. None of today's "preparations" that people fear will be useful nor applicable.

It is actually God who engineers the conditions necessary for the antichrist's accession to power (covered also in *Revelation the Fair God*). Satan never wins. History proves it. Noah's family and the beautiful animal species did escape: Satan did not win then. Later, Pharaoh's systematic killing of the Hebrew boys did not prevent Moses from living and conducting his appointed task at the right time: Satan did not win. The killing of all the babies and toddlers around Bethlehem did not prevent Jesus' ministry and task: Satan did not win... And the list goes on. Satan will rule unopposed after the rapture only because God will have removed His direct presence (Spirit) and His own people (saints). God abandons the losers into Satan's hand.

1. God made man in His own image; neither man nor Satan will be able to dehumanize the whole of humanity in such a way that a person is not a "human-with-a-free-will" anymore (as these Globalists' control measures attempt to make us). We must remember that the people who follow Satan are wrong by definition; so we cannot build our reactions or chart our life on their affirmations. Let us stop building on this sand castle! During the three and one-half years of testing (the span of time we call the great tribulations), the eternal choice will be demanded of every living Gentile—every one of them with his God-given capacities intact. The people facing the stark choices that will control their eternity will still be unmodified humans, the way they were divinely created. The mark of the beast on the individuals will not be applied on a population of re-engineered robots. The obvious inference is: today's New-World-Order and its human-altering plans will have to be destroyed in our time, <u>before</u> the great tribulations begin. This is because Satan does not trigger the "tribulations"; God does, and the human-altering plans of the Globalists will not be a factor then.

2. During the rule of the antichrist, people will not be chemically or genetically induced (controlled) to make the fatal choice for the mark of the beast. No-one's mind will be controlled remotely and driven to be marked like a programable automaton. Right after the rapture of the

believers, two of God's angels will make two things very clear to all living (Revelation 14): Jesus is the only way to blessed life eternal (so choose to die in Jesus) and taking the mark of the beast guarantees you unbearable, unending and unabated suffering. It is with these understood information that each person will make his/her choice—in many cases under duress, but yet not controlled. As far as I can see, this is non-negotiable. Again: all the cyborg and trans-human threats will have to be vacated before the rule of the antichrist begins.

3. Here is a reality many "Christians" I know fail to realize: The antichrist will not rule because he won the position. The antichrist does not conquer. God wins. He completes the harvest and takes the winning team up with him (rapture). God vacates the field and turn the Satan-devoted losers over to the ruthless treatment of Satan and his antichrist. Followers of Jesus: take heart! It is God's actions that makes it possible for the antichrist to step into the ready-made circumstances. God is not backed into a corner.

4. If the humans, during the "great tribulation" were not free-willed creatures anymore, why would God address every of them through the two specific angels above (Revelation 14) at the beginning of the antichrist's rule? It would be nonsensical for God to address these people if humans were already under the chemical/genetic control of the antichrist's system. If humans did not have a <u>real</u> choice, wouldn't it be silly for God's angels to preach to them? (For an in depth study of this process, please read *Revelation the Fair God*.)

If humans are to remain good-old-fashioned humans, then I propose that the obvious recalibration of our thinking must be: The Globalists' New-World-Order/One-World-Government and the controls they project (Deep State) will have necessarily failed (or have been destroyed) prior to the advent of the antichrist. The Globalists will have been defeated prior to that time. Their manipulations will not be a factor; no matter how ominous they appear to us today.

In short: Since we are in the times of the end as foretold and described by Isaiah, Paul and Peter, the One-World-Government/New-World-Order will be destroyed in our days—and this means very, very soon.

No wonder the Globalists and their puppets (Deep State) are frantically over-reaching: they have become desperate. They are doomed and their master Satan knows it.

So, if the Globalists and their patsies are routed and destroyed, it begs the question: who destroys them? Will God destroy them? Or will the good people rise and do it? And what will this do to the United States of America as we know it?

The answer to these questions were my earnest prayer. I wanted to know so that I could align with His plan. And God answered: He will do it. He had told everyone a long time ago in Daniel chapter 2.

Daniel 2, the destruction of the fourth empire

A historical, geopolitical overview before delving into Daniel 2

At present, from a citizen's point of view, our personal and national outlooks seem grim and hopeless. In our present world, the "good" is crushed and does not have a chance to prevail anymore; the bastions of our collective well-being have been dismantled. The optimists among us rally behind hopeful cries of: "Let's vote the ruffians out and elect in good people". The realists say: "Yes, we'll vote: but there is no assembly of men today who, when in place, will have the fortitude and tenacity to root out the rot". Or: "There is no voting out the immense, entrenched, unelected and ultimately self-serving governmental administrative legions who draw secure, generous salaries leading to an assured golden retirements; they are the real control. They are committed to perpetuate the gravy train they are on." There doesn't seem to be an "America" anymore.

What happened? Traditionally, the society of carnal men organizes itself under a leader—usually a king or an emperor. Since the fall of Adam, the masses of men do not do well when left to their individual devices. This has always been true even when the people had received clear directions from God through Moses, as witness: individually, the Israelites could not live according to the divine principle given them (read the book of Judges). Their mindless, headless and fickle meanderings are pitiful to read about. They did not want to be individually responsible; so they begged for a king. The king did not solve their condition: a king is never the answer for the human condition. Humans were created in God's image; to be guided divinely. Any other way will leave a lot to be desired.

The answer to the condition of every human is God. Humans were not made for a horizontal, inner-species deflection of responsibility. So, while "good" kings can help; "bad" kings multiply the problems—and historically, there has been far more "bad" kings than "good" ones. Power corrupts, absolute power corrupts absolutely. And, when a man gets power; he will strive to keep it and secure it; thus he will always entrench it, buttress it and increase it; moving further and further from the Godly ideal of personal, vertical responsibility.

God created man to be individually responsible and vertically led. The average man shirks this God given reality. We tend to choose fear and cowardice over the noble attributes of our creation. And as someone wrote: Once you reject God, you are fated to try to replace him. We do not remain godless; in a most pathetic way, we will always subject ourselves to a "god" whatever it is.

> <u>Note:</u> Horizontally, at man's level, every individual is always responsible. This never goes away. It is so clear that in the old testament a person was to be held accountable for damages done inadvertently—let alone willfully. Vertically, we are created to be led by God at all times, moment by moment. Jesus' principle is: Follow Me. We are not created to be led by people. Asking for a king was always wrong for this very reason: it violated the vertical component and deflected the horizontal principle. Deferring to a human power as it applies to the direction of our life is treasonous to God.

A couple centuries ago, very bright men and women who had a deep moral compass, an overarching respect for God, rightly conceived a republic of individually responsible men managing their affairs and the affairs of state. Theirs was a unifying effort built on the common strength of their Christian faith. The concept was that individually responsible, vertically led men could manage collective life.

They were very clear, though, that this "magnificent experiment" could only work, and its principles could only operate if the Christian ethic, Christian faith and Christian commitment remained the rules in the people's individual hearts—independently from the organizational headship of their religion. They understood that the commitment had to be personal for the system to work, so they legislated against a Government imposed Christianity. They were right: only in Christ, with His Spirit motivating the individuals for the good and toward God, can man live an upright life—personally first, then collectively. The founding fathers rightly understood that if—or when—this active foundation eroded; the population would be in the very same morass the early Israelites were after they received their God-given land and bungled it badly. So, on the premise of a nation made up of God-following individuals the United States of America were born. The process was never easy because the base reality of fallen humanity is a very heavy stone hung on the neck of everyone and it threatened to crumple the effort at every turn.

Not surprisingly, at about the same time the early Americans were working on their unifying construct for their emerging country (based on the strengths provided by the Christian faith and principles), there arose in Europe a Satanic/Luciferian system of world control—antipodal to the American concept and antagonistic to Christianity. It is a construct of world domination, a universal empire, if you will. This evil construct is based on promoting and exploiting the basest attributes of the fallen human nature for the purpose of elevating an elite by enslaving the masses using money, greed, absolute selfishness and ruthlessness. Its strategy, tactics and operations are divisive and destructive. It is totalitarian in every way: it aimed to rule every country, and to control everyone in all the countries, to own and manage all resources and to dictate what the people can believe, what they can say and can aspire to. Today, we have a name for this evil empire: the Globalist One-World-Government/New-World-Order, an evil order born of the secret societies. We saw some of its facets on the world scene over the last century: Communism. Communism is the scion—a limited and partial application—of the Globalist One-World-Government/New-World-Order. Communism was the overt transformative step in some parts of the world while, under the radar, the empire decimated and weakened the rest of the countries through profound corruption. Daniel 2 describes this supra-national fourth empire and places it in our time.

With a driven resolve and an absolute absence of compassion, this satanic cabal has systematically wreaked havoc on countries and peoples. Here is a sample of their doings: They were the instigators, the movers and arbiters of the first French Revolution (1789 – 1793). Their aim and purpose was to destroy France as a country. To savage her economy and in the process to annihilate as many French people as possible. And using the same blue print; they went on from there, systematically savaging countries and peoples.

From what I have read, this fourth empire was the brainchild of Mayer Rothschild who in 1773 convened the main family pillars of the Illuminati to create the resources and impetus for "a new world order" (imagine that: a New-World-Order!) Adam Weishaupt was tasked with expressing the tenets and acting principles of this empire. It is sometimes referred as the Weishaupt code. *World Revolution: The Plot Against Civilization*, distills the Weishaupt code this way: *the abolition of inheritance, of marriage and the family, of patriotism, of all religion, the institution of the community of women and the communal education of children by the State...*

Today, none of these tenets have changed. We can plainly see them all around us. And they are being imposed upon us with great severity and unbending dedication.

This evil agenda does not change—even down to details that we think are details of our modern time only. For example, within the goals of the French Revolution there was an official program of depopulation (They spelled it dipopulation). They wanted two-thirds of the French population eliminated. They preached that the land of France could not support the level of population it had then (24 millions); but could only accommodate 8 millions... today this fourth empire's message is the same; but it is global: the earth cannot accommodate its current population and the growth thereof. (The phoniness of their arguments is revealed by history: without ever suffering from famines, France still over produces food for its now 60+ millions inhabitants!) The reality is: God created the universe and put man in it. The God-made universe will always sustain human life. Until GOD extracts the humans and destroys this universe.

Back then, during the revolution, a committee in Paris met everyday and went through lists of inhabitants of provincial towns, and marked those to be killed. These were drowned, or guillotined. Drowning and guillotining are slow processes, which were hardly efficient for depopulation; so only 300,000 marked people were thus eliminated. (By the way, only about 3,000 were from the nobility, the other 99% were basic population; so much for the "proletariat" propaganda.) The French Revolution was never the spontaneous uprising of the oppressed we were taught in school. It was always orchestrated by an elite.

Almost a century later, in the late 1,800's, one of this New-World-Order organs of publications—the *Freiheit*—rejoiced thus: "...*Science now puts means into our hands which make it possible to arrange for the wholesale destruction of the brutes in a perfectly quiet and business-like fashion...*" Man's tools for killing had improved by then. Imagine what they can do today with modern mass murder delivery systems, the global killing capabilities that are available to them?

Right from the beginning, well over two centuries ago, this evil cabal banished God from France and they imposed a complete pantheon of man-designed idols that represented and served their cause. Does this seem familiar to us today? They called it reason then, now they call it science.

They turned men against women and vice versa. They invalidated marriage. They isolated the children from their parents; the children belonged to the state.

They winnowed out capable, intelligent leaders and replaced them with second rate intellects and corruptible—yet proud—blockheads. They did this at all levels of leadership and administration.

They created the welfare state... and then—as always—they failed to provide for those who depended upon it... The Deep State of the New-World-Order have never delivered on anything helpful or uplifting; their goal is destruction. None of their policies have ever worked. As Daniel 2 says: they *shatter and break everything*. And right from the beginning, the New-World-Order turned its destructive efforts against the nascent United States of America. It had no trouble finding an "elite" that embraced their evil agenda and imposed it upon the people.

Since 1789, beginning with France, The New-World-Order elites pushed socialism, especially state socialism and yes, they even promoted communism, using these exact terms (add an "e" at the end and you have the original French words). They manipulated the rabble into demanding the abolition of national government... just as they still manipulate our rabble today.

They systematically hewed down the national character of the population; just like they do today. And, just as they do today, they planned on using fear to dominate the lives of the gullible "government-free" people. It still works today: billions of people hunkered down in fear in their dwellings during COVID's well-organized fear campaign. And weak-minded people today are still reticent to start living fully again; by lingering fears or by self-consciousness: because it would be a confession of their gullibility and mass idiocy. They would lose face (the face they learned to hide behind the absurd mask). This global, satanic cabal de-humanizes the populations.

Over time, this same fourth empire engineered the Bolshevik Revolution that began to neutralize the great popular advancements the Russian monarchy (especially Alexander) was initiating—and was working hard at implementing: the liberalization of the people and the end of serfdom. The aim of the Globalists is to enslave the masses; not to emancipate them, Tsarist Russia had become a threat to them. If the Russian masses were emancipated; the Globalists rhetoric would be a dead issue. These same Globalists evil actors frantically derailed these Russian reforms and went on making slaves all across that large land, they starved the masses, killed the masses, and misled all... The Bolshevik Revolution and the ensuing Communism was the outreach of the Globalist Empire. This fourth empire *shatters and breaks everything*.

For the Bolshevik Revolution, the globalists behind the scenes, used the same template they had used for the French Revolution. First, they destroyed the monarchy, when this was accomplished, they destroyed the class that had the capital, they called that class: bourgeoisie. With the destruction of capital and the leadership of the country vacant they could now enslave the people. Which is what they did. They shatter and destroy everything. They systematically "beat" God out of the people.

And in between these revolutions, the same cabal sponsored the American Civil War, fomented the destruction of our union using our corrupt and naive politicians and generals. So; right from the early days over two centuries ago, the fight was on. The powers of darkness have incessantly attacked every pillar of our American foundation. Today, the powers of darkness overtly declare themselves the enemies of all Godly directives and principles.

During the 1920'S the very same group destroyed the German spirit, the German family, the German faith and pushed all the degrading vices the Globalists' LGBT+ are pushing today. German society never recovered; it is terminally warped. During the next decade, sponsoring the NAZIs, this Fourth Empire ossified the deconstruction of the German Christian life through the awful period of 1933 – 1945. The German people never recovered their spiritual foothold.

This fourth empire successfully uses two types of grifters to promote and enforce their power. They masterfully use the greedy, self-advancing political opportunists who are receptive to the State Socialism rhetoric—as long as these leeches expect their future position to be among the lording elite (Think: Politicians, judges, church leaders, university faculties, military brass... and any other grant-sensitive grifter in any field). And, second, they arouse and manipulate the anarchists who just want to destroy and have no real interest in what would naturally come after destruction is wrought (Think: Antifa, Black Lives Matter...) Both groups—the State Socialists and the anarchists—have historically been grifters par excellence. They are parasites. They are our banes; but their comeuppance will come alongside that of their hidden masters.

There is one more characteristic to this empire (the Globalists' One-World-Government/New-World-Order): it is the ever-present connection with the occult. From its inception, the occult—that is: the satanic—was, and remains, the connective tissue of this empire's many iterations. Which makes us realize that *our struggle is not against flesh and blood, but against the rulers, against the powers, against the worldly forces of this darkness, and against the spiritual forces of wickedness in the heavenly places* (Ephesians 6:12 TLV). Our attitude must not be to ignore its realities and certainly not to appease it. But to personally arm ourselves with the armor specifically provided for us and equip ourselves with the sword of the Spirit which is the word of God... and to stand, and stand, and stand! We are not provided with tools to out-politick them. We are not encouraged to outsmart them at their own game... The reason is; we won't have to: God will face them and destroy them.

A century ago, *Nesta Helen Webster* brilliantly brings our attention to the plight of the Deep State instigators (New-World-Order/ One-World-Government) who lamented about their lack of penetration into the life of the people of England at that time. She wrote: *And today, Lenin has declared the greatest obstacle to the success of Bolshevism in England to be the fact that the English working-man founds his ideas upon the Bible. If the people of our country* [England] *will but realize the diabolic nature of the conspiracy at work amongst them, the power of Hell cannot prevail against us. In ignorance and indifference lie our principal danger. Every outbreak of the World Revolution that has so far occurred has been rendered possible by the apathy of the* [targeted] *nation in general.*

How true!

This was England in 1920. What about America in 2020? What is different one century later? Nothing: The Satanic/Luciferian empire has continued unabated, fomenting wars in many places, destroying societies. So one can wonder: will the vicious, destructive cycles continue forever? No, they will not; because during the last decades we have entered the *latter days*, the end times of our era. The conditions laid out more than two millennia ago have arrived—as we will document later in this text. Evil is now "out of the closet" ; it is overt just as it was in Noah's time.

Today, on a pedestrian level, the Globalists seem to have their programs all but completed and their controls all but absolute. Caving to them, the United States of America is now a dim shadow of what our proud country used to be, stood upon and projected—and what it could have been; but did not become. Divorced from our foundations, we are free-falling and there is no bottom in sight. The valiant and noble hopes the country once entertained have disappeared. This is man's pedestrian view; it is how it used to appear to me.

So, when down; look up! Do we have a reliable reference point, outside our circumstances and fears, that could cue us about what is happening at this specific time in history and what will happen?

Yes, we do. God planted specific markers for us. As I review these, I will be stepping on cherished theological toes; but you the reader should decide. The main texts I will use are Daniel 2, Habakkuk, Jeremiah 50 and 51, and as cross reference, Isaiah 47.

Let us take historical stock: Where are we, historically? Or in other words: Are-we there yet?

Our days on the timeline of history

We are at the "time of the end" Daniel speaks of in Daniel chapter 2. I am convinced that we have entered this final period already because Paul (in 2 Timothy 3) and Peter (in 2 Peter 3), described for us the particulars that would define the time of the end. As you read these passages, imagine yourself walking through your city, shopping at your stores, trying to educate your children or watching our mass entertainment: You will recognize that the harbingers Paul and Peter gave us are all around you. Aren't these foretold conditions the realities of your world? So, assess today's world and decide for yourself if we have not already eased through the threshold of that time unawares—into this final stretch. This is for the secular side.

On the spiritual side, ponder the following considerations. If you are a follower of Jesus, put on your Christian lenses and read Paul again: *Remember this! In the last days there will be many troubles, because people will love themselves, love money, brag, and be proud. They will say evil things against others and will not obey their parents or be thankful or be the kind of people God wants. They will not love others, will refuse to forgive, will gossip, and will not control themselves. They will be cruel, will hate what is good, will turn against their friends, and will do foolish things without thinking. They will be conceited, will love pleasure instead of God, and will act as if they serve God but will not have his power. Stay away from those people. Some of them go into homes and get control of silly women who are full of sin and are led by many evil desires. These women are always learning new teachings, but they are never able to understand the truth fully.* Paul is talking to the church about the "Church"—the last three verses make this abundantly clear. Look around you; look at your church, look at your denomination, your mega-church, look at the church at large, the clergy in general... We are there, aren't we? We cannot look at the world, call it bad and feel insulated. All the deviances Paul lists, and all the reproaches Jesus lists in the first three chapters of Revelation, are present today in the church, they are accelerating and are becoming generalized. We are there; this here is the state of "Christianity" in our day.

Our falling short, our progressive moral regression does not hamper God. His plan and His schedule will be carried on regardless of our position or readiness.

And for God, the time of the end is also the period of fulfillment of momentous prophecies when He reveals his majesty and power through sweeping actions on this earth. It will create conditions on earth that we have not seen in millennia. What are these divine events of the "time of the end"?

1. The destruction of the fourth empire, followed by
2. The final exodus of the righteous Hebrew people toward the land of Israel, followed by
3. The battle of Gog and Magog, that will segue into:
4. The seven years of God's rejoicing with His ancient people in Israel, and finally, to end our common era:
5. The glorious, peaceful rapture of the true followers of Jesus of all times.

Within this progression, the marker that is instantly discernible today is number 3: Gog and Magog; because its circumstances are easily identifiable. It is the only one that seems to have a "perishable date" on it. For example, we can easily identify the supra-national empire of our time as the Globalists' One-World-Government/New-World-Order and we can easily see how long it has been in operation. However, by studying it, we cannot tell if we still have decades to go—or even longer—before Jesus destroys it. But when we consider the Gog and Magog event from our slot in history, it seems that it cannot be delayed for long. It is a tangible vector that bisect the march of the Globalists' Empire.

Gog and Magog can happen either through a political and military coalition or simply under the banner of a Turkish leader. We often assume that each of Ezekiel 38's listed regions is led by it own king/government. But is it what the scriptures say? Let's looks at these possibilities.

Gog and Magog was inconceivable when prophesied by Ezekiel: At that time, there did not exist a multi-national coalition consumed by hatred against the Hebrews and Israel. But much later, from the latter part of the seventh century, there has been a body of people dedicated to the destruction of the Hebrews: the Moslems. However, there was no country of Israel against which they could rally and carry out their prophet's commands. But that changed: In our time; "Israel" as an entity exists. Some Hebrews do live in Israel now: this is condition number one for Gog and Magog. So, since 1948, the possibility of Gog and Magog taking place is real. However: when?

If the battle of Gog and Magog is waged by a coalition of countries; can it happen in our time? Yes, it can: An unlikely coalition has taken shape today. For 25 hundred years this assemblage did not exist; but today is does. I write "unlikely coalition" because the two main kingpins of the coalition: Turkey and Iran, had been systematically opposed to each other for millennia. Even when their Islamic religion should have united them; they chose opposing factions that have been in internecine war with each other. Their enmity goes deep. But recently, they act in concert and cooperate with each other. They have an alliance. But age old enmity like theirs does not die easily so this coalition cannot be sustained very long. It has to fulfill its purpose soon—or it must dissolve.

Then, to complete Ezekiel's prophecy, two other countries that have had no polarity in that area—Sudan and Libya—have joined Iran and Turkey; just as predicted. It seems that the unlikely coalition foretold in Ezekiel now exists and therefore God could activate the prophecy at anytime.

On the other hand: Does Ezekiel describe a coalition, or, can the battle of Gog and Magog happen under the banner of one Turkish leader? Yes, it can happen under Turkish leadership.

Ezekiel describes an assemblage of regions not a cooperating league of leaders. The "Stan" republics (plus Azerbaijan), from Turkey to China, are firmly in the influence sphere of Sunni Turkey. They are united by their traditional languages, their ethnicities and their religion. What Turkey says; the "Stans" hear. To my vantage point: these are the lands that form the northern cap of the territories listed in Ezekiel 38—not Russia.

So, a political and military alliance of Turkey and Iran may not even be necessary for the momentum of Gog and Magog to take place. But the population in the land of Iran will be involved. The text of Ezekiel 38 only mentions one leader: Gog—not a coalition of equal leaders.

Looking at today's geopolitical situation, we may only need the implementation of the greater Turkic/Ottoman Empire—from southeastern Europe all the way through the asian steppes, to the border of China. That is the revival of the great Ottoman Empire so dear to Erdogan. And this is not far fetched.

In that case, we increasingly see that Armenia, the tiny, Iran supported, sliver of territory is the plug that stands in the way of the ambitious pan-Turkic Ottoman Empire. This is an aggravation to them: Turks must cross other countries (Georgia and Iran) to get to these "Stan" republics and vice versa. That lack of control and access is a huge impediment to the Ottoman ambitions... So, Iran must go.

All that is needed is for Turkey—or some other factor—to sabotage the government of Iran, create political upheaval or a change of regime. So that Iran becomes another destabilized, rudderless land of Islam from which hordes of Jihadis can flow into the battle against Israel under the Turkish banner.

The scriptures seem to favor this possibility, as it only speaks of one king, of one leader—a Turkish one: Gog of Magog. This is the leader

God-Almighty will forcefully bring to battle by putting hooks in his jaws.

Besides the regions of Turkey (Gomer, Togarmah), the text of Ezekiel 38 lists the other areas: Persia, Ethiopia and Put as the geographical—not the political—sources of this great flood of Islamic soldiers. All the Moslems in these territories, answering the call of Jihad, could come out to fight under the banner of the Gog of Magog (Islamic Turkish leader). So, Gog and Magog may not require a coalition of governments. The territories listed in Ezekiel 38 might just be the areas from where these soldiers will come.

If this is the case, then the battle of Gog and Magog can readily happen at any time. The vast Asian lands of the Turkic "Stans" are already tuned into Ankara. Muslim bigots of Iran, Ethiopia, and Libya do not necessarily need their own domestic government to answer the Jihad call. So, let's keep an eye on specific developments in that area.

> Note: Russia is not part of Gog and Magog. For a few decades, we, western students of the scriptures saw Russia as the kingpin of the Gog and Magog coalition. We were lured into this thinking because our perspective was based on the USSR, instead of on historic Russia. We concentrated on the new and alien communist reality that was anti-Jesus at its core. We failed to see that the USSR was first of all anti-Russia at its foundation and for its motives.

> Russia, a mostly Christian country had been moving toward the same God-given individual rights based society as America's foundation was. This was a direct threat to the Globalists' One-World-Government programs; the evil cabal focused its ire onto Russia. Russia was derailed, the wonderful progresses were eradicated and the country was

almost destroyed by the Luciferian construct of the USSR. The propaganda motors within our own society conditioned us to see Russia only as USSR (a product of the Globalist Empire) and to hate everything Russian. We believers should have known better. This anti-Russian mentality is now deeply rooted within our society, our organs of power, and even in our pulpits; it blinds us.

When the communist construct imploded, chaos followed, but then, after a few years, Christian Russia rose from the ashes and is now blooming again. Russian society began cleansing itself. Today, it shames us; its laws are moral—ours aren't. And more significantly for Gog and Magog, Modern Russia has shed its Muslim territories; territories that will participate in Gog and Magog. Indeed, all the "Stan" republics are almost completely related to Turkey by their languages, ethnicities and united in their anti-Israel religion; these republics do not affect Russia anymore. It seems that God freed Russia from the twin evils of Communism and Islam; just in time for Gog and Magog. He separated His own; He spared His followers. The belligerents of Gog and Magog will be drawn to the hills of Israel by God. It seems that He has set traditional Russia aside from the ill-fated coalition.

So, for the first time in history, the battle of Gog and Magog is the reality on our horizon. This means that the other events that precede it must happen presently. Are we there yet? Yes, we now are.

The destruction of the fourth empire

According to Ezekiel's text, before Gog and Magog takes place, God will achieve exodus 2.0: the extracting and culling of all descendants of

Jacob and their transfer to their promise land. This poses a dilemma for the geopolitics of today: If one ethnic group is affirmed and subtracted from the control of the Globalists, then the One-World-Government concept crumbles. And even worse, when this God-led event happens, the God of the Bible will be permanently established—thus invalidating all their efforts to dethrone God. The Globalists would be done for.

Furthermore, from my work in Israel, I was made very aware that the Globalists control the country and its politics. So, logic demands that something drastic must happen to these people before God brings His remnant into the land He will give them again.

The God of heaven and earth has identified and addressed this issue of our time and specifically foretold its process through Daniel (2:28 – 45).

For the old testament, Daniel 2 is an oddity because it does not seem to be a Jewish-centric prophecy. It is odd also because it has no relevance at all for the people of Nebuchadnezzar's time or for their Canaanite descendants. Plus, it is unique in another way: no one was querying God about the subject. And God was not reacting to a gross iniquity there. The prophecy is unilaterally introduced by God (a dream) and clarified by Him. Its message precedes man's perception of a need for it. As Daniel says: the king had been musing about the things to come and God laid out a vision far beyond what man could have sought then.

In this prophecy, God clearly identifies the Globalists' New-World-Order/One-World-Government of the last two centuries and gives the divine script for its destruction. The die was cast more than two millennia ago. The text is clear: The Globalists are doomed. Using the TLV reading, this is what it says:

28...There is a God in heaven who reveals mysteries. He has made known to King Nebuchadnezzar the things that will happen in the latter days...

29 To you, O king—as you lay on your bed—came thoughts about what will come to pass in the future. The Revealer of mysteries has made known to you what is going to happen.

*... 31 You looked, O king, and behold, there before you stood a huge statue—an enormous and dazzling image, whose appearance was awesome [**frightening** (NCV and others)]. 32 The head of that statue was of pure gold, its breast and its arms of silver, its belly and its thighs of bronze, 33 its legs of iron, and its feet partly iron and partly clay.*

34 While you were watching, a stone was cut out, but not by hands. It struck the statue on its feet of iron and clay and smashed them. 35 Then the iron, the clay, the bronze, the silver and the gold were crushed together, and became like chaff from summer threshing-floors that the wind blows away. Not a trace of them could be found. Then the stone that struck the image became a great mountain and filled the whole earth.

36 This was the dream. Now we will tell the king its interpretation. 37 You, O king, are the king or kings to whom the God of heaven has given sovereignty, power, might and glory. 38 Wherever mankind, beasts of the field, and fowls of the heaven dwell, He has given them into your hand, and made you ruler over them all. You are the head of gold.

39 Now after you another kingdom will arise, one inferior to yours. Next, a third kingdom, one of bronze, will rule over all the earth. 40 Finally, there will be a fourth kingdom, strong as iron—for iron shatters and breaks everything—and just as iron smashes everything, so will it shatter and crush all the others. 41 Just as you saw that the feet and toes were partly potter's clay and partly iron, so this will be a divided kingdom. It will have some of the strength of the iron, for you saw the iron mixed with clay. 42 As the toes of the feet were partly iron and partly clay, so *this kingdom will be partly strong and partly brittle. **43** Just as you saw iron mixed with clay, people will mix with one another, but they will not adhere to one another, just as iron does not mix with clay.*

***44** Now in the days of those kings, the God of heaven will set up a kingdom that will never be destroyed, nor will this kingdom be left to another people. It will crush and bring to an end all these kingdoms. But it will endure forever. **45** For just as you saw a stone cut out of a mountain, yet not by hands, crush the iron, bronze, clay, silver and gold, the great God has made known to the king what will happen in the future. Now the dream is certain, and its interpretation is trustworthy.*

What do you think?

Here are some salient points:

The statue was extremely visible: it was huge, it was shiny; impossible to miss. It was also very frightening. This verse tells us the following: people in the world were and will be very aware of the overbearing presence of each of these empires during their own eras. We will develop this in the paragraphs below.

The kingdoms this statue represents are also frightening. This is an important detail. These kingdom were not—and will not be—benign. And indeed, during Daniel's life, or Esther's, we can see that the central power had no qualm killing people, even entire ethnic populations. Esther, the king's favorite bedmate was very frightened at the thought of approaching the king uninvited. If you stepped outside the central will, your life would be worth nothing... and the lions would eat well!

So, these kingdoms will strive to maintain and increase their ostentatious reach (the statue was huge), their ostentatious riches (the statue shone) and they will project fear (the statue was frightening).

These four kingdoms are world-wide kingdoms. *Wherever mankind...dwell, He has given them into your hand* tells us that the first kingdom was universal as far as far as the population of that time understood. Punctuation in other translations makes it clear that the second and third of these kingdoms *will rule over all the earth* also. From its inception, the kingdom of our time has set itself to be the universal empire that rules over all the earth—the One-World-Government. There are no parts of the world where its rule does not exist. Territorially, the Globalists One-World-Government/One-World-Order is a world-wide construct. (Heretofore, the "kingdom" of our time will be written as fourth empire.)

When will the fourth empire take place? The God-given information: "*finally*" (or "*the latter days*") is specifically given for the benefit of the people of our time so that we—who recognize the latter days—can make use of the knowledge early and in real time. It is meant to be useful to us; so we should make use of it. (There would be no reason to mention the timing if we could only be aware of it post-history: it would be of absolutely no value then. The value of a "heads-up," of a warning, is in advance of the event. We expect a speed warning before a dangerous turn; we don't need it after the turn.) As mentioned above, I believe we are in the *latter days*; there are no subsequent chapters of traditional history left so the fourth empire is the kingdom of our time.

Note that the first three kingdoms have value. The text represents the values as gold, silver and bronze in descending order—interestingly, we can readily relate to this ranking: we use it in many value rankings (like the Olympics' gold, silver and bronze). Because they had intrinsic value, these kingdoms could be "builder's" kingdoms. In their own way, they promoted or facilitated the corporate life for their people. But the fourth empire does not have intrinsic value. Its nature (iron) is identified by what it does: it smashes and destroys. And in time, it rusts, it corrodes down to iron dust. It carries its own destruction within its molecules. This fourth empire does not "build"; it destroys. And as laid out in the text above, the Globalist cabal has systematically demonstrated these traits everywhere it chose to strike. It has never built; it has only undermined and destroyed what was built. And as noted above: this empire is frightening and relentless. The hundred of millions it killed and their families would attest to this.

These four kingdoms are not godly kingdoms, even though the first was endowed by God of certain qualities and prerogatives. Each will strive for absolute control of their world, but being human (and Satan led), these empires will never be able to defeat the kingdom that God will set up during the time of the last three human empires: *The God of heaven will set up another kingdom that will never be destroyed or given to another group of people. This kingdom will crush all other kingdoms and bring them to an end* [Jesus, the Rock, will destroy the fourth one], *but it will continue forever... You saw a rock cut from a mountain but no human being touched it. The rock broke the iron, bronze, clay, silver and gold to pieces* (verses 44 – 45).

Jesus is the God who set up His own kingdom after the first (Nebuchadnezzar's) but during the span of the last three. This tells us that empires two and three are contiguous with Jesus' era and Christianity. And the Rock who sets up His lasting and superseding kingdom is the divine agent who will destroy the fourth when it is time to do so. Jesus, the Rock, began His kingdom during the Roman Empire, an empire that exhibited the traits we discussed above. It seems logical to consider the Roman Empire as empire number two. (The New Century Version is the easiest to read on this passage.)

Each of these empires left a human "heredity" in their wake, so traces of each are still present through later history, even today. Modern states were established on the principles of these empires. Their laws, their structures of government and even their architectures have been carried over. Some modern republics have judiciary bodies called Senates, their official buildings often reproduce the styles of these past powers, some heads of state were called Kaiser, Czar (Caesar).

On the evil side: The fourth empire, the one in our time (the latter days of the text), is strong (overbearing) because through corruption and the corrupt-ability of the elite it vies to control everything and everyone in a strong-arm manner. This is what the Globalist One-World-Order is and what it does. But, it is brittle...

Indeed, its only medium is money. It has no intrinsic value like the other empires had. It never creates conditions that will be universally useful. It does not promote the natural coalescing of the people; on the contrary it divides people to weaken them.

Money is the weakest mechanism of control. It is the control of the parasites; not of the producers. The Globalists (and their Deep State) produce nothing and provide nothing—<u>they never have</u>. Thus, their control can be broken <u>instantly</u>. It is brittle.

A second aspect of this empire is division (feet of iron mixed with clay). This division is the direct consequence of its composition. People brought together for money, and through the love of money (and power) are selfish and by nature, they are social climbers (they climb over other people to get what they want). They always pursue their individual selfish aims and gains. So, while the Globalist One-World-Order talks a united game, its players and proxies, are not united. There is no "us" with them; only a bunch of mercenary "me's". Their "unity" is only cosmetic. Their commonality is superficial and contrived.

This division is the fruit of the natural limitations imposed by the fourth empire's evil nature. Their master Satan is not a manager; he is a destroyer, so theirs is a permanent juggling act with constant fallouts.

Also, the tiny group of evil men at the top could not, by themselves, overwhelm and rule the masses everywhere and all the time. They needed a large manpower base. Yet, at the same time; they do not want to share their ascendency. So, to project their control and to progress their agendas this tiny group had to "bring in" a legion of cadres in all aspects of government (kings, presidents, congressmen, judges, policemen, union officials, administrative workers , etc., plus petty, unprincipled anarchist agitators)—they are the Deep State. These numerous, heteroclite people share the same motives: they are very selfish, self-serving, deceptive and corruptible. So, even their own motives divide them. Observe them: they are not just "me first"; they are "me only".

Money does not buy loyalty: it only rents it. When the money stops, the rented loyalties vanish. There is no cohesion amongst all these traitors and snakes. They flow together only as long as they float on the common funds given them by their manipulators. So, while these numerous cohorts of evildoers join hands and forces, they are never united. Any real threat to their bribe supply or to their personal safety will make them scamper. Any harsh and profound upset would send them splintering away—each for his own. Real courage—the upright kind—is not found among them.

Also, this large, multilayered cohort never feels truly secure in their positions or assured of their usefulness because the upper elite uses them and then, with total callousness, discard them. These bought minions never reach the inner sanctum of the cabal. Because of these factors, uncertainties and fears dominate their lives; they are forever striving to buttress their position, to secure their status. Their untamable fears make them murderous toward outsiders whom they perceive to be a threat.

In the end; they remain useful idiots. Idiots because they are deluded and think that their "services" have earned them immortality within the system. However, since they do not produce anything; they would be the first to be destroyed should the cabal reaches its goal of total control. Ironic, isn't it?

One hundred years ago, Nesta Helen Webster recognized the weakness as she quotes Barruel: *Keep yourselves* [good people], *however from giving way to that kind of terror which is cowardice and discouragement; for, with all the certainty of the danger, I say to you nonetheless: 'will to be saved and you will be saved'... One cannot triumph over a nation that resolves to defend itself. Know how to will as they do and you will have nothing more to fear from them.* And Barruel wrote this a century before Nesta Helen Webster wrote her own book—that is to say: two centuries ago. The Satanic/Luciferian plot has not changed, the playbook has remained the same; and today, it is imposed on us all as well. On the positive side, the advices of Barruell and Nesta Helen Webster still apply.

> <u>Note</u>: I only quote Nesta Helen Webster in this essay within the narrow context of Marxism/Leninism expressed above. I wholly condemn her antisemitism. I do not subscribe to her views in that respect.

When we consider the French Revolution, we see that this Satanic, secret cabal could never unite the masses into following them. This cabal could only push people into believing certain lies and committing certain actions; but they could never generate a lasting following, a loyalty. They could not generate a self-propelled spirit of permanent changes. How could they?

This tiny group of elites was invisible, acting from obscurity, it was never recognizable—people cannot identify with something they cannot see! People proved that they will not trust a group they do not see, a group that is never identified at the personal level. So in the end, the Globalists only created lasting pains, lasting destruction, lasting disunion; but they never gain the voluntary joining of the people. The cabal never offers a spontaneously unifying platform. By their actions the French lost their soul, but never built a transforming cohesion. Ever since, the French have milled around, accomplishing nothing.

The fourth empire had to spend all their energies to keep their many revolutions going; and every time, in the end, they ran out of steam, the momentum died, so they regrouped and tried again... the pool of corruptible patsies ready to take their bribes never runs dry yet it never develops an independent, self-sustaining momentum.

In the prophetic image given by Daniel to Nebuchadnezzar, the tiny elite at the top provides the iron (the impetus for destruction), and the descending orders of cadres form the clay. These two components need each other but they cannot depend or trust each other nor can they coalesce into a unified force when adversity strikes. The tiny elite despises the venal legions they continually purchase; while, the corrupt, moral prostitues believe they have attained inclusion, but the corrupters despise them for their demeaning, slavish weakness.

> <u>Note</u>: The descending orders of cadres are the ones who perform the actual evil dictates ordered by their handlers. They too will bear the guilt of the destroyers.

And this is precisely what will happen when Jesus (the stone) strikes their edifice. They will shatter in millions of pieces! It is not just their corporate structure that will be destroyed; it will be every atom that makes it a body politic. Each person will scatter. But, this will not spare any of them. Jesus will be thorough: they will all, every one of them, be destroyed in the manner that fits their individual guilt. There will not even be a trace left of them or their systems.

When Jesus-the-Rock acts, no one will be able to attribute the actions to any human factor or endeavor. And the change will be permanent: the stone (Jesus) remains on the scene to grow in stature and become the only supra-national power for the remainder of our era. There will not be a rebirth of the fourth empire or the rise of a fifth empire of that type ever again. We are at the fulcrum of history.

Finally, before taking a look at the details of all of this, there is one obvious conclusion to be made. While this is a destroying empire—a construct that gathers selfish people without uniting them—it also constantly seeks to bind the masses at large into submission by creating mass fears, universal fears. God did say that the representation of these empires would be frightening. And the one of our time is particularly frightening because it has the technology to monitor us intimately.

The fourth empire of our time cannot provide the masses with an upstanding or righteous ideal and agenda to embrace—unlike the founders of our country did. So, to carry out their control agendas, all they can use is fear. (No wonder in the Bible God clearly commands us over and over again: do not fear!) For a long time, the fourth empire used wars almost exclusively to create fear; but now universal, instant, mass communications give them the means to readily impose any type of fears abroad the whole earth. They can globally control the narrative and keep fears alive. Viz. the earth is cooling, we are all going to be dead by (insert the date)... The earth is heating up, we are all going to die by (insert the date)... The climate is changing, we are all... This pandemic will kill millions... Those who do not do what they say are condemned as selfish at best or mass-murderers at worse—So we are told...

The bible teaches us to live life to the fullest (John 10:10). To personally stand on God's promise. To face fear yet to believe and to strike out with confidence. All this is absolute anathema to the cabal. How can they abide a God that commands every follower "do not fear" when their only tool to control the masses is fear?

This explain why any patriotic movement is an existential threat to them—because by definition a patriotic movement unites people and it moves them forward! A patriotic movement is something individuals can embrace and become self-motivated about. This is why the cabalists systematically and frantically attack and attempt to destroy leaders like Trump, Bolsonaro and Orban (and yes: even Putin). These have successfully stoked the patriotic, unifying spirit of their people. If you want to identify who has been bought by the evil empire in our country: watch for those who opposes and disparages the leaders above and the nascent patriotic movements that born them. This is why the Globalists do not want borders, or nationalities: they aim to eliminate anything that might unite us. Anything that might give an identity to our "us".

Finally and above all: This cabal must kill Christianity because true Christianity aims to empower the individuals by bringing them in the company of the God who created them. And true Christianity aims to train the persons to be all they were meant to be—individually responsible and vertically led. There is no room at all for a Satanic empire in Christianity.

And Christianity is the indomitable kingdom that begun during the second empire. It is the kingdom whose king will destroy the Globalists' empire as well as any trace of the preceding world governments. Satan has read Daniel 2. He knows whence the destruction of his edifice will come.

Jesus confirms Daniel 2 very precisely in Matthew 21:33 – 46. The leaders of the fourth empire in our time have definitely adopted the motto: If we kill the son, we will inherit the vineyard [the world].

They truly strive to "kill" Jesus and the idea of Jesus as well as suborn the Christians and their way of life in order to establish their claim of a "New-World-Order"! Even the choice of the name of their endeavor—New-World-Order—indicate the change of ownership they strive for. And as Jesus fittingly says: "*Whoever falls on this stone* [Jesus] *will be shattered; but the one upon whom it* [the Stone] *falls, it will crush him.*" What God revealed to Daniel and confirmed through Jesus' own words will indeed happen to end the fourth empire of our time.

Opposition to Jesus and persecution of His followers has always happened; but until now, it was more sporadic. It was not globally coordinated, not set as a universal goal. It was not overtly and purposefully aimed at stealing the world from its Creator—totally and permanently. Today, the conditions outlined by Jesus exist. It is time for the Stone.

> <u>Note</u>: The Globalists are robbing all of us of everything we have, they tax us as if they own us, and finally, they plan to rob God Himself of His possession—dispossess Him of the work of His hand! Just like the men in the vineyard of the parable.

The doomed supra-national empire

God will finally and completely destroy our current Globalist One-World-Order; we, who live today, will not have to accomplish this. Let's look at Daniel's text.

This prophecy bridges over most of history, from the Babylonian Empire to today. It addresses a specific type of empire; a type that will appear only four times.

> Please note that this Babylon, or Babylonian Empire is not the Babylon of the tower of Babel. The Babylon of the tower

of Babel is the subject much discussed in the last 18 chapters of Revelation. But it is not relevant here.

Also, for the sake of simplicity I lump together the Canaanite Babylon with the Babylon of the Medes and Persians that segued directly. I do so because Jeremiah 25 does not make a distinction between these three successive kingdoms: Canaanite, Mede and Persian, as he gives us a one stretch of seventy years for the exile of the Jews under these successive kingdoms. So the Medes and the Persians are not empires two and three of Daniel 2. And as Daniel says: in the times of these kings (second to fourth) God will set up His kingdom; so the second through the fourth are contemporaries of the Christian era—Rome may be the second one.

This here document is not a historical research into the second and third empire. Daniel gives no identifying details for these empires so that we are not distracted from the point of this prophetic dream: which is the fourth empire. And this fourth and last empire is well defined in the text because it needs to be readily identified by any reader of scripture. It was scheduled for our time.

As far as I understand, the Babylonian Empire was the first true world empire; a decidedly supra-national entity. In Esther, we are told that it extended over 127 states. It dominated, managed and taxed the developed world of that time. It ruled a multitude of peoples and languages. We know that each of the four empires shown to Nebuchadnezzar in his dream will be a world empire in its time because Daniel reiterates this characteristic for the third kingdom.

> <u>Note</u>: Other kingdoms had been established at earlier times; but they were far more restricted in reach (such was the case of Egypt's pharaonic kingdom in Moses' time). In some translations of this passage Daniel addresses

Nebuchadnezzar as king of kings because he ruled over many regional rulers (local kings).

The Babylonian Empire had specific, defining attributes. It effected its power and authority from the top down; it was not a representational system. All the channels of power and authority were vertical and centralized. People in position of authority were appointed from above; not elected from below. People who became useless or cross to the system were discarded or eliminated. The Globalists' One-World-Government/New-World-Order functions the same way.

The Babylonian king made the laws. Legislative bodies—if there were any—did not make the laws. Advisers may have proposed ideas for laws; but only the kings made the laws. Today, only the very tiny elite at the top of the fourth empire sets the directives and ensures the enacting of the laws.

There was also another distinctive and defining trait to the Babylonian empire: it did not just civically administer and militarily protect its people and lands; it vertically imposed and/or prohibited religious beliefs and practices. Through various biblical passages, we read that its king commanded all the people to worship the God of the Hebrews, while at other times, the king commanded by decree and under penalty of death the worship of a statue of himself, and at another time with the same conditions to pray only to him...

There was no protection of religious beliefs from the control of the state and the state did not grant individuals the liberty of worship—or the choice of deity. Does this begin to feel or look familiar to you? Isn't this what we have progressively transitioned into? The Babylonian State used the full weight and power of its crown and institutions to impose what people must believe, how they should think and whom they may worship—It enforced political correctness. And as we see in various parts of the book of Daniel, those dictates were subject to change as the power on the throne followed its own whims. Does this seem familiar?

Left unchecked by God, the rulers automatically veered to the occult, to Satanistic idolatry. We can watch the process through the book of Daniel. Each time, they did this, the rulers were chastened and realigned with the All-Powerful God. Why did this happen this way? Because God's chosen people lived under the absolute power of these monarchs, so God put barriers and divine recalls to protect His people.

The fourth empire does the same thing: it promotes every possible rebellious, idolatrous and devious beliefs and practices. Satanism (the worship of Satan to pursue every degradation possible) and Luciferianism (the worship of Satan for the pursuit of power and godhood) are welcome and protected. It is focused on destroying all Godly matters and principles. This empire will be destroyed by God/ Jesus... Because it knows better; so its waywardness was an informed, willful and systematic pursuit of evil.

> <u>Note</u>: This top-down sponsorship of spiritual dogma should not be confused with countries and regimes that have an official state religion (as are found in historical Catholic kingdoms or in Muslim nations). In these cases, the religion predates the state and is the power over the state and through the state. The state simply sanctions and defends the religion it serves; but the religious prelates make the spiritual rules. In this construct, there is a continuity of beliefs that are not subservient to the state nor subject to who is on the throne. The temporal power does not change the religion.

> In contrast, in the Babylonian empire, spiritual laws and the sanctions attached to them came down from the king and not from a religious entity. There was no continuity

nor oversight provided by an existing, independent spiritual reality.

We will show that the Globalist Elite's power over societies is similar to Nebuchadnezzar's in each of these areas: Its governance is not elected, it rules by diktats, its small central core makes all the rules. And it also imposes what the people can think and say, what they may worship and what concept of the divine is acceptable... And they punish—or demand that their vassals punish—all diverging positions and actions.

Finally, the Babylonian Empire had voided all organized opposition from within. When we read about Meshach-Shadrach-Abednego or later Daniel we can see that there was no existing, organized resistance or opposition to the unfair, sacrilegious dictates of the state. These righteous individuals had to take their own personal responsibility and to face the peril of the state on their own. The state had "rigged" all the avenues of power and to power. Can you see the parallels?

This is what I see in the world today: The Globalists' repression of Christian thoughts, principles and practices. The repression originates with the state. De facto, as Americans we are not a "Christian nation"; we are a godless state where some Christians live. Do you see it?

The Globalist cabal imposes what we can think and believe as serves their purposes. And they mean to severely prosecute dissidents. Just like Babylon did, they control and impose their own spiritual orthodoxy independently of any religious concerns. In short: They are gods... And they overtly say so: One of their foremost thinker and influencer; Yuval Noah Harari, titled his new book *Homo Deus*—the man-god.

Today's fourth empire *à la* Babylonian Empire has "rigged" all avenues of power and to power. They absolutely control, from the inside, all the political parties, agencies, courts, associations, most of the churches, etc., so they can concentrate and apply their ire and punishment on each of the lone individuals who valiantly take their personal responsibility seriously. Like the three Hebrews and Daniel, these individuals bear the brunt of the vindictive apparatus, and pay a price far greater than the "insult" warrants. It is a frightening system.

Today, unlike the Babylonians, we have the illusion of choice; but not the benefits of the choices. This is what I mean: if one side of the aisle is in power, and their decisions and practices offend us; voting for the other side does not bring any changes. They are sides of the same coin; a coin controlled from far above the peons we see. And as things go these days, the powers are getting bolder and soon, they won't even need to provide the illusion of choice or of freedom to maintain their grip on their empire. They will have completely boxed us in regarding all aspects of life. They will have reached the full level of control and threat Nebuchadnezzar enjoyed.

And like its ancient Babylonian model, the current Globalists' "empire" rules over many countries and it rules vertically from the top. Its higher echelons are not elected; they are put in place. There is no representation from the masses and of the masses (more on these points later). Governments that stray are replaced from above.

It is fitting that the Babylonian empire should be the first world empire on Daniel's list (the head of gold in the dream): it displayed the combination of all the above characteristics. It serves as the prototype. These defining characteristics and their context make the fourth empire of today the evident heir of the Babylonian empire.

While of the same type of empire as the other three (supra-national and spiritual), the fourth differs from the others by its origin and outcome. The first was established by God and granted authority by Him—the text says so. It was likened to the head of gold. Gold is the noble metal by excellence. It is the symbol of honor, blessing, stability and of collective recognition. Gold was used for vessels of service and honor.

Gold has intrinsic value. That empire passed away of natural wear; its dominion unsustainable.

On the other hand, the text does not tell us that the fourth empire will be ushered by God nor established by Him: it will just appear—that is: God will allow it. It will not be made of noble metal (or I should write noble mettle). Iron is hard, traditionally it is the metal used to make crushing tools, hammers and such. Iron can also be tempered and sharpened and made into killing weapons of war. By nature, this empire will destroy (crush and kill); Satan begot it, and he is called the destroyer for good reasons.

But, unlike gold, silver and bronze, iron is itself subject to self-destruction by corrosion (corrosion: think corruption). Corrosion's effects are hidden at first, not easily detected until the ravages are so extensive that they become apparent—and permanent. And sure enough: Our fourth empire began its work in secret darkness, and grew its influence behind the curtains; in the back rooms of power. And today, the rot is becoming apparent to all. The corruption cannot be hidden anymore.

The fourth empire also diverges from the first in one significant aspect: it is Jesus—the Stone-not-cut-by-human-hands—who will destroy it. It will not pass away in history in a natural way as other human endeavors do. The power of the Globalists will not fade in history; it will be destroyed by God. An event to be witnessed by every living person of that time. It was God who effectively favored the first of these empires, but it is God who will dramatically end the last one.

It makes sense that only a direct Divine intervention can put an end to this empire; its reach is so pervasive, so complete that humans cannot deal with it. Indeed, neither a person—nor a group—could scour out the rot. No one can wade successfully through the layers of lies that implicate his own family, his friends, his own town, state, his clubs and associations, his church, university...every agency that governs his life... Humanly it could not be done.

This is how I understand the prophecy of Daniel 2; what do you think?

Today, the Globalists' New-World-Order is truly a power in the lineage of the Babylonian empire; it is the "daughter of Babylonia" as predicted in Isaiah 47 (NLT). From its secret, dark, and underhanded inception, it has functioned from the top down. It first corrupted the kings whom it enslaved through debt, and through the kings it enslaved their peoples. The way I see it, the approach was astute: kings and politicians do not produce anything at all. This means that they have no personal means of leverage whatsoever. Their control is money and the military enforcement that money can buy. The Globalists offer both these components of power... and in turn these provisions guarantee the enslaved indebtedness of the masses who have to bail out their kings and their politicians; a proposition these moochers find hard to turn down.

As I look around and talk to people in different lands, I see that the Globalists' Empire controls many lands today and rules peoples of many languages; just like the first empire did. Its programs and interventions touch every continents and every land in each continent. It erases old boundaries and mercilessly herd people into new ones. It vies to control the food supply, the health solutions, the population densities and every other aspect of life. It imposes its rules over local government and tells them how to enforce the One-World-Government centralized diktats—abortion, environment, climate change, thought police...

I also see that the Globalists are at war against Christianity, against the God of the bible as well as the followers of Jesus. Jesus' is the competing kingdom; the kingdom God began with Jesus and has kept alive since then. The Globalists' repression and banishment of Christian thoughts, principles and practices originates with the state. I see this as a very telling parallel to what the Nebuchadnezzars did. The Globalist cabal imposes what we may think and believe as serves their purposes. If we disagree, we are branded enemies of the people or even terrorists and are penalized or punished. We live in a world of instant dispersion of information, the present, odious empire can project the images of its punishments and killing to the whole earth, multiplying its frightening effects.

I think Christians are becoming aware of the relentless pressure applied against them—its effects were so progressive at first that we-the-people did not become aware of the process for a long time. We fell for the emotional "good", the societal "nice" and we left the biblical "right". Unaware, we yielded to the incremental pressure. We have tolerated their points of view (they make us feel ashamed if we do not), they progressively modified our beliefs in accordance to their agenda; so, now: Pure, unadulterated Christianity has become strange to most of us. By and large, we have become "church-ians"; we are not "Christ-ians" anymore.

Beyond the various kings and the political elite, the Globalists corrupted European theologians, then universities, then clergy... (add your own observations to this list). This elite has warred relentlessly against the God of the bible, against Christian thoughts and against the Christians themselves. But this Globalist cabal does so independently of any established religious tenets—just like the Nebuchadnezzars did in the Babylon of antiquity; they make their religion as they go. In short: They are gods.

These aspects are major factors that identify the fourth empire of Daniel 2 as the Globalists' One-World-Government/ New-World-Order. It is the same type of empire; thus, it is the one we should watch out for.

Timing is everything

We know when the first of these empires existed. We are given no indications regarding the timing of the second and third. But, for the fourth and last empire, Daniel 2 gives us a black and white time slot: it will be in *the latter days* or the *time of the end,* or also: *finally*. It is for now. So, are we there yet? Yes, we are.

Additional details about The supra-national empire of today

The first empire—Babylonian Empire—is the prototype, the one we can study, learn about and compare with to identify the others. As such, it is well documented. I cannot speculate what the second and third of these empires have been (the empires of silver and bronze); they are not relevant to us today because we have entered the *"finally"* of the *latter days*. Therefore, the last empire, the legs of iron and the feet of iron mixed with clay is the geopolitical reality of our time. This fourth supra-national empire is indeed the Globalists' One-World-Government/New-World-Order.

As Daniel explained to Nebuchadnezzar: God will not use humans to destroy this empire, He will use the *stone not cut by hands* (Jesus). God will share neither the credit nor the glory.

The Globalists' One-World-Government/New-World-Order that increasingly dominates and chokes our lives is only legitimate by substitution but it is very real by application. By substitution, I mean that when they hand down laws and dictates, these come through the apparatus of "our own" governments and are enforced by our own governments and their local administrations; even though they come from a centralized "higher" source—this is a substitution of power and authority. As good citizens, we feel bound to obey and respect the laws we are given because we do not see whence they originate and whom they serve. We submit because we believe that we are deferring to our legitimate government. Recently, though, the Cabal has become brazen and demands that national authorities be surrendered to them in all matter. They are becoming more and more overt.

The Globalists' One-World-Government/New-World-Order looks for and pursues what it can get dishonestly, it is even willing to kill a lot of innocent people to get it (abortion, euthanasia, endless wars, artificial famines... these are the killing attributes of sharpened iron) and the Cabal feels free to hurt people (financially, medically, socially... the crushing attributes of the hardness of iron) and to steal from them. It is a truly barbaric empire. It serves its master: the destroyer.

Like the Babylonian empire, the fourth empire rules over many regional and national powers—because it owns them (it corrupted them and bought them on the cheap using their own debt-laden monies). It has hidden in the shadows, it still shuns the light, but it controls ruthlessly. Like iron, it is corroded (corrupt) and it corrodes (corrupts and compromises) everyone and everything it touches. Like iron, it has been used for destruction—as in destroying nationalities, morals, natural law and to kill massively through endless wars, abortions and euthanasia...

It has ruled because it relentlessly divides the masses. It banks on and exploit selfishness in the people it targets. Every attribute of life is used as a dividing factor. They have succeeded because so few people are anchored upon the word of God. And among the ones who know the true God, fewer yet apply the principles in His Word. Few believers discipline themselves according to the unflinching precepts of God. Many believers practice casuistry at some level. The Globalists have succeeded because Christians, by and large, do not want to live the independent and personally responsible life that their submission to the vertical authority of God demands; they want the comfort of a group; the support of a cohort, and thus they are easily manipulated. Man was created to be personally responsible on the horizontal plane and vertically led. In the image of his Creator, he was made to be courageous and free (courage being the management of fears—not the absence of fear).

Corroded iron never has a positive outcome: it deteriorates into uselessness and finishes as rusty dust. Fittingly, this empire will end pulverized into dust blown by the wind. This Satanic fourth Empire has consistently removed all possible good outcomes for the populations it controls, and it has sabotaged hope. Its latest slogan says that if you forgo everything that you hold dear, everything of value, and relinquish the last strands of your will; then you will be happy.

The Globalists' New-World-Order projects an abject, useless death for all. It has spread its pall of darkness over all. It demoralized the masses. The minions of these elites have relentlessly pumped messages of doom. Remember: The earth was cooling, we were all going to die if we did not heed their policies. Then the earth was warming up at an alarming rate, so we were all going to die if we did not heed their policies. Now the earth's climate is simply changing... so we will all die... The earth cannot support today's population; so billions will die (even though we over-produce food and the major health hazard is obesity)...

> Note the absence of basic logic: the argument is that the earth cannot support 8+ billion people therefore we must preemptively kill the "surplus". Their solution is: let's kill the billions we deem to be excess population! Is that asinine or what? Why not wait and see if God's earth is indeed inadequate to supply the needs of all the people God gives life to? Why not let an all-knowing God take care of removing the excess population? Why go by the ever

changing whims of dimwitted "scientists" and "experts"? So, even their basic premise makes no reasonable sense.

They browbeat us down, saying: If we do not submit, humanity is done for. But if we do submit, what we get is so foreign to good life that there is no hope in it—every aspect of your life will be monitored and sanctioned, you will own nothing and you will be happy...eat bugs and artificial food... (why artificial food? Because if man makes it; there is no point of thanking God for it!) This is not life. And certainly not the "life more abundantly" that Jesus promises.

Regarding artificial food: The curse was that Adam and his descendants would have to work hard and sweat for their food; but the food would still be provided by God, through God's controlled nature. God never relinquished His control over food. Food is the ultimate control. Substituting artificial food for real food is the latest attempt at wresting control from God. Partaking in such a food is a voluntary slap to our Maker. Don't do it!

> <u>Note</u>: Following the rapture of His saints, God will turn off the spigot of His natural generosity and no new crop will grow (until Jesus' 1,000 year reign). And would you know it: the harsh metering of what foodstuff is left over from the generous preceding seven years of the great harvest is the very control the antichrist will use on the hapless, defenseless and guilty population. This is what the black horse of the Apocalypse lays out for us and what the second angel preached. The message then will be: Hungry? Get the mark and you will get your daily food—albeit never enough. Eat bugs? Indeed...

As the prophecy says: this empire *shatters and crushes all the others*. It operates without pity or empathy, with an iron grip through bought operatives whom it assiduously embeds in all posts through which authority is dispensed (Deep State). Its rule is pervasive, it dominates and dictates its will in-and-through every world organization.

The fourth empire builds on illusions. It does not even use real money; it makes up its own money. This sham money costs the elite nothing. Then the cabal artificially charge the little people an ever increasing real price of sweat and tears for it! It reflects its master: Satan is the deceiver.

This empire-in-the-shadow was never elected, it was never desired by the people; yet it taxes, punishes and ostracizes. It imposes an orthodoxy of thoughts and it polices the beliefs that it promotes and it criminalizes all other beliefs. This self-proclaimed elite claims to own the all the God-provided resources of the planet—even the air we breathe—and presumes to have the exclusive right to regulate and allot these resources. As I wrote above: they are gods. More than merely being the masters, or stewards of the universe; they claim to own the universe. No wonder they will be crushed when the real, legitimate owner of the universe has had enough of their posturing. Then everyone will discover what Nebuchadnezzar found out: *God does what he wants with the powers of heaven and the people of the earth. No one can stop his powerful hand or question what he does* (Daniel 4:35 NCV).

Who gave these tyrants these rights? No one; their narrative is empty and relies only on their ability to lie and threaten. They nurture fear in the heart of the weak-kneed populations. And as easily observed: the "Christians" in our western societies have become gutless. We crave ease; not value. They have shamefully bought the lies. The Bible commands us not to fear...for a very good reason; fear opens the portal into every life.

This evil cabal controls the information media and thus shields the people from accessing the truth. They have instituted a circular sink hole for information: false scientists float a scary lie, then from their side of the court, the press broadcasts it, citing "a reliable scientific source". Then the false scientists build on the first premise citing in turn the press "discoveries" as basis to do so. It would be funny if it were a child play. As it is: it hurts millions of gullible lives every time they float a narrative. The other aspect of controlling all information, is that it precludes freedom of thoughts and independent decision making. And finally, the Globalists' dictates ignore the local rules of law.

Within many countries, the operatives of the Globalists' One-World-Government run the executive branch of government. The Global elite owns the monarchs where monarchy still exist. It projects its control from top down. The Global elite has established a controlling influence in the various legislative bodies, the justice systems, administrative offices, national and regional agencies, the press, the academia, school systems, the militaries and the CEOs of the multi-nationals of many countries—ours included.

Who are the top leaders of the cabal? Who is, or who are, the emperors? I don't know. I can only see the lower tiers closer to me.

Who will be spared the suffering when the fourth empire is destroyed?

The ones who follow the true God in Jesus will be spared.

At the pedestrian level of the people, there is a significant population who have embraced Jesus and who follow Him. They do not mix nor give into the Satanic doctrine being forced upon them. We can look at many geographic theaters where the Satanic empire of the Globalists rules and we find an irreducible core of uncompromising Christ followers. Take China, there are now more than one hundred million Chinese followers of Jesus. They are true followers; they have to be because otherwise they could not press on under the terrible persecution by the state. Take Africa, thousands are coming to Jesus every month, under sharp and unrelenting persecutions by the local Moslems. Indonesia, has stopped publishing reports because the Christians now comprise more than 15 percent of the population—in an officially Muslim country! Latin America is experiencing a shift from Catholicism to Bible believing faith. We will look at the USA further down in the text.

These two populations—the fourth empire operatives and the true Christians—cannot both prevail. Therefore, we who search scriptures must understand the play at work here.

Like in the parable of the wheat and the tares, the wheat does not try to overpower the tares (it is not its task to do so); but the tares aim to overpower the wheat and choke the life out of it. The tares were purposefully put there by enemy of the righteous Master to try to drive the good crop asunder. But it will fail because it is not meant to succeed. The good crop is alluded to in Daniel 2: *During the reigns of those kings, the God of heaven will set up a kingdom that will never be destroyed; no one will ever conquer it.* Eventually: *It will shatter all these kingdoms into nothingness, but it will stand forever* (NLT). This is God's Kingdom.

The good crop's task and purpose is to <u>be</u> the good crop, to develop as the good crop. In the end, the harvest does not happen because the good crop has eliminated the tares. The harvest happens when the good crop has reached maturity. The good crop does not vanquish the tares; the Master's crew will do that. We forget this principle. We, believers, must steadfastly concentrate on being the good crop. Jesus said: *Follow Me*, and He prayed that we may *be wherever He is*; so let's concentrate on this. The Rock will destroy the false crop.

And to the point: The tares, the false crop, never overcomes the good crop—ever. In the end, the false crop fails; it fails to overcome the good crop and it is destroyed by the Master's crew. All during the extended maturing process, the good crop keeps growing, keeps maturing, keeps bearing the promise that was assigned to it.

Please note: the harvesters do not cause the harvest to grow and ripen; that's God's job—this has always been the principle. The harvesting crew gets in motion when the Master of the Harvest says so. The Master of the harvest sends the harvesters; Jesus says so: *There is such a big harvest of people to bring in. But there are only a few workers to help harvest them. God owns the harvest. Ask Him to send more workers to help gather His harvest* (Matthew 9:37 – 38 ERV). It has always been the case.

God gave us the Good News and all the teachings of Jesus. And then harvesters of every generation went to work. The good crop has never been so successful as it is now, never been so close to maturity and plenitude. And in our time, the growth and ripening of God's harvest will be further energized and multiplied by an infinite factor through the witnessing of <u>God's spectacular, universal, actions</u>: Divine destruction of the Global power, followed by exodus 2.0, followed by Gog and Magog. We, disciples of Jesus must be prepared to work in the train of it.

> Please note: Our commission is to make disciples of Jesus and to teach them all Jesus' commands—that's the harvest. The actual transformation of the believer happens at the personal level. It is never a group thing. It is a factor of the converted soul's personal and sustained responses to God's feeding and leading. Most institutionalized churches, by making "churchians" of us, stunt—and mostly bypass—this intricately personal process of the new life.

Back to Jesus' inspired analogy of the wheat and the tares: The enemy will always attempt to drag us into a direct fight against his tares—against him. He banks on our sense of propriety and of being offended by the evil he demonstrates overtly; but it is a taunt. In the parable, when the tares were discovered, the crew were offended, but the Master held his crew back, because they could do more harm than good if they went after the tares. The Master knows that the good crop WILL bear its promises, regardless of the tares. Being lured by the enemy's moves simply derails us into a battle we cannot win; because it is not our battle! Jesus said: "follow me"; not "fight the windmills of the enemy".

The Satanist Global agenda has not succeeded in completely steamrolling over the world because, by their mere existence, the true disciples of Jesus occupy their assigned ground... And the Master watches over the good crop. The presence of the kingdom that God has set up is the impediment. And the Globalists cannot fix this anymore than the tares could prevent or nullify the harvest. Nothing can stop God's kingdom.

The Satanist cabal thinks that they will eliminate the minority that does not submit to their evil god. But it won't happen. Instead, the Stone, the champion of the Christians, will destroy the fourth empire and its construct. We often hear that: "in the end God wins". This is not quite true: all through the process, God is in control and He will carry out His agenda of divine feats just as He foretold it. So, it is not "in the end God wins"; but it is: God is on His way to victory all along. This is not a Rocky Balboa scenario when the hero is beaten up badly to an inch of his life but blindly land a final lucky punch. No; God has won every round and will continue to do so.

The harvest of the good crop does not take place because the tares have made it impossible for it to thrive any longer. Not at all: in spite of all their invading ardor, the tares have not prevented the good crop from prospering and reaching its full maturity. The tares lose. The Master knew it from the beginning.

In the end God wins...because He has worked it out that way from the beginning and controlled it all the way to that end. The apostle John tells us that before the world began, God willed Jesus to be and to save. As Jesus says: do not fear; just believe.

> Note: The destruction of this empire is corroborated by Isaiah (45:20 – 25) *The LORD says, "Come together, people of the nations, all who survive the fall of the empire..."* For the Gentiles, this post-empire process will be the "great harvest" (see elsewhere in the text).

Let's look at the divine events that are on the cusp of happening.

The sequence of God's march of glory

God's March of Glory is my own expression. It is my personal take on a sequence of events that have been promised by God and will be carried out directly by Him. Chronologically, these events are: the destruction of the fourth empire, followed by exodus 2.0 (this time it will be a worldwide exodus: from every country of the world into the land of Israel). Then, Gog and Magog will follow, ushering the seven years of God's rejoicing in Israel, and eventually the rapture of the believers. Nothing will derail this...Even though sometime, at our level and from this side of it; it seems impossible.

This march of glory will change life on this planet. Conditions have not happened in this way since Man could walk with God in the cool of the day in the garden of Eden. Imagine: everybody on this earth will actually see God/Jesus as He carries out His universal interventions. Everybody will have seen God. Most will not yet personally know Him

(His personality and traits); but all will witness His reality and many will query about Him... and this is the very purpose of it all.

God provides the tools of discernment by clearly identifying the fourth empire in Daniel's text. As previewed above, God gives us two traits and a historical marker. The traits are: Iron with its forceful destructive effects, and iron mixed with clay with its divided fragility. And God specifies the time of history: *the latter days* (or the last days)—the days Peter and Paul described clearly for us to identify. Thus, equipped with the timeframe and the distinctive characteristics; future believers could recognize this fourth empire and would know when to look out for it and what to look for. And today, we can do both.

Biblically, there are very few events left on God's prophetic calendar. It seems that these events are tightly grouped into a space of 9 to 12 years as they all segue directly from one into another. The matter is developed extensively in the books: *The Great Harvest of the Post Allah World* and *Revelation the Fair God*. But in short, here is the run down of this chain of events (what I call God's march of glory):

Event number one: the very visible, very graphic destruction of the most powerful, most ubiquitous and invasive human machine: the fourth empire (One-World-Government/New-World-Order).

This results in the first universal reality check: God exists and man is no match at all for God. God beats man... Even man's most powerful empire ever.

Event number two: very soon after event one, God will extract every descendant of Jacob from every country in the world and after a brutal and exacting culling will, in full view of the whole world, lead the remnant into Israel. Everybody in the world will see the God of Israel act and judge omnipotently. As we will develop later in the text these first two events may be part of the same process.

This will result in universal reality check number two: The God of the universe is the God of Israel.

Event number three: This exodus 2.0 will be followed shortly by the destruction of all the false gods of the world at the battle of Gog and Magog. By destroying the Muslim armies that will attack Israel, God will remove all presumption of Allah being a god at all. Isaiah 46:2 will come true for all to see: *The gods cannot protect the people, and the people cannot protect the gods* (NLT). This will create a universal spiritual vacuum. Again, the whole world will watch this divine, history-altering, action in real time on their phones, tablets or computer screens. Isaiah 44:9 – 20 tells us that *all those who make idols are worthless... those who worship these gods are blind and ignorant—and they will be disgraced... Every one who worship [a false god] will be humiliated...* What a real shock this will be for more than a billion followers of this false god. And what a wake up call for the followers of other lesser gods.

This will result in universal reality check number three: there is no god other than the God of Israel.

What will be the impact of these successive divine events on the people? Man is no match, God is Israel's God, no other god exists... How will this tweak the people's perception of life and their theories of the supernatural? What will it do to all the human constructs of the afterlife?

(Today, Gog and Magog cannot be postponed for long because the incongruous coalition listed in the Bible now exists—so the battle looms on our horizon. Which tells us that exodus 2.0 which precedes it must take place very soon indeed. And the destruction of the fourth empire must precede the actual exodus 2.0.)

I understand that the subject of the timing of Gog and Magog is controversial with many (pre-tribulation, mid-tribulation or post-tribulation advocates). However, none of the theories I have read about and none of the arguments presented make much sense. I will not develop this point thoroughly here since I have done so in *The Great Harvest of the Post-Allah World* as well as in *Revelation the Fair God*.

Item number four: As covered in Ezekiel, Gog and Magog will be followed by seven years of rejoicing in Israel when all the living descendants of Jacob will get to know and worship Jesus the Messiah—the Messiah they have now seen in action at the destruction of the fourth empire, then at the extraction of the Hebrews and the judgment of the rebellious, the actual exodus, and then the incredible crushing of Gog and Magog. This is the full and complete harvest of the Hebrews. The reciprocal, or parallel, effect for the Gentile world outside Israel will be the largest harvest of souls of all time, because every Gentile will have seen these world-changing actions of God/ Jesus. Of course, not everyone will come to Jesus.

The result will be the universal reality check number four: The question on billions of people's mind will be "Do you know this God and can you introduce me to Him?"

Event number five: At some point when the 7 years promised to Israel in Ezekiel have been expended, and the final Gentile who will embrace Jesus freely has done so, Jesus will take up His faithful followers to be with Him at the magnificent, peaceful and most awesome event of all time: the rapture of the saints of all of history. Indeed from Paul's letter we can deduce that one day, the last person who would voluntarily embrace Jesus as LORD and Savior will do so. When that happens, the harvest that begun at Pentecost will be over. A special dispensation will be provided for the living Hebrews. 144,000 will take part of the rapture and the rest will be taken care by God in a safe haven and later will live in Israel—as normal human beings—during Jesus' 1,000 year reign. (Their transformation and rapture will come at the end of this reign.)

God's team vacating the field will be a universal reality check for the losing team: Sorry; you are now on your own!

From this parade of divinely gratifying events, and right on the heels of the glorious rapture, God will impose three and one-half years of testing to the Gentile, anti-Jesus, crowd. He will do this by abandoning every Gentile into the hands of the antichrist and his master Satan.

This is the reverse effect of the march of glory when God reveals Himself and His attributes. Following the rapture and God abandonment of the people to the god they chose; these souls will have a rude epiphany: how miserable life is when God has pulled out. Since good had not convinced them; the contrast with overt evil might convince some yet. And so it will be.

The few who refuse their doomed destiny and renounce their prior allegiance to evil will be beheaded. Jesus, the Savior of the world, will gently pick up these post-harvest "gleanings". They are the last Gentiles let into a blessed eternity.

When the last gleaning has been picked up, God will hit the earth of the rebellious Gentile humanity with the greatest series calamities ever experienced—save for the flood. This phase will be kept short (somewhere between 6 to 6 ½ months). God will whittle down the world Gentile population to the ones who will be the servants of the Hebrews for the 1,000 year earthly reign of Jesus. The cabal who aims to depopulate the planet today, will probably be part of the depopulated crowd! Poetic justice, or: be careful what you wish for...

Jesus' one-thousand year reign will follow. This earthly millennial reign will then segue directly into Jesus' eternal new creation. You can find a realistic scenario of what life will be for remaining Gentiles in *Justin's Tomorrows*.

As for presently: The imminent universal change that Jesus brings through the destruction of the fourth empire is permanent and applies through the rest of history. Daniel's text says *the stone that struck the image became a great mountain that filled the whole earth... The God of heaven will set up a kingdom that will never be destroyed, nor will this kingdom be left to another people.*

From the moment *the stone that was cut out from the mountain but not by hands* crushes the feet of clay and iron (that is: Destroys the fourth empire), Jesus rules, period. His kingdom was planted long ago, year by year, century by century it has endured and grown; it is close to maturity in our time.

This changes everything.

There will never be another supra-national empire/empire. Jesus' kingdom began 2,000+ years ago and since then people everywhere could join in and belong; but now it will reach its purpose.

The points above challenge the assumed scenarios we read about and are preached on: We are told that, the first massive intervention of Jesus will be when He comes near—in the clouds—to lift up His followers of all times at what we call the rapture. No one outside His followers will see Him that day. Just as no one outside Jesus' followers saw Him ascend on the day of His rapture (the prototype for our own rapture). Following the mass rapture event, the accepted scenario tells us that Jesus will come back after the "tribulations" to reign with an iron scepter for 1,000 years from Jerusalem with the complete retinue of his faithful followers (Revelation 20:4 – 6). This simplistic view does not take in account the old testament promised events. It does not account for Jesus' direct action as the stone. And it does not provide for all the promised revealing of God to all in Ezekiel, and several other prophets.

Note: The "tribulations" is a brief hiatus when God/Jesus withdraws the access to Himself to the Gentile humanity. He will not answer prayers at that time, He will not mitigate evil, He will not interfere with the beheading of those who choose to die in Jesus. He even removes the bulk of His witnesses from the world: the believers and His spirit, leaving only two human witnesses in Jerusalem. Jesus tells John: *Whoever is to be a prisoner, will be a prisoner. Whoever is to be killed with a sword, will be killed with a sword* (Revelation 13:10). There will be no divine mitigation: whoever accepts the antichrist's rule will be deprived of all freedom, rights and decency with no succor from God. And whoever then chooses to die in Jesus will have to go through physical death without the divine comfort the martyrs of the Church age receive. This is why they are urged to endure: they are alone in their trial.

In Daniel, we are clearly told that Jesus, who destroys the fourth world-power in our time, will become the permanent supra-national power from that time on. He will not do so physically—as in His visible, touch-able resurrected body—but through His Spirit as Jesus has done since Pentecost and since His own rapture (ascension). Something to think about, isn't it? Plus, Ezekiel and others clearly say that every living person will see God/Jesus effecting exodus 2.0. We need to rethink our cultural theology: What we have been preached does not fit the whole of scripture.

The globalist's supra-national empire of today fulfills the prophecy

As developed earlier, more than two hundred years ago, God allowed the fourth empire, the one we groan under, to be secretly conceived and put in action by a cabal of thoroughly wicked people (some say Satanists/Luciferians) who set out to dominate and rule the entire world by corruption and violence. They aim to eradicate God. Their intentions were never noble and their practices never are either. To reach their ultimate goal of total global power and control; they have systematically de-humanized the masses, removed decency, identity and especially hope. They did this in France 230+ years ago, they did this in Russia as well as in Germany from early twentieth century on and they are doing it now to the USA and to the rest of the world. Early in their conquest, and within a short time, they successfully subjugated all the Western regional powers using the tools of money and the greed of their patsies.

In the beginning, these evil actors were invisible to the masses, few people knew of them or understood what was happening. To this day, most history books, most school curricula do not document their role nor their responsibility. These evil conquerors seemed patient—it was not patience; it was thoroughness. They were the effective power behind the curtain. But recently they have become rabid, they are not hiding anymore. They want to bring their masterplan to its desired conclusion—now! Not content with ruling the world, they are eager and impatient to be worshipped. They are trying to race God and derail His march of Glory.

Why are they in such a hurry now? Could it be because their prophesied end is near? And because exodus 2.0 is coming soon? Why does exodus 2.0 present a danger for them?

Let's look at the prototype. In Moses' time, the Egyptian monarchy and administration opposed the first exodus. In our time, it is the Globalists who will be the power who would want to oppose God's transfer of every Hebrew from every country into Israel. So, the Globalists' power will be broken prior to exodus 2.0.

Beyond this terminal loss of face and credibility, just as in Moses' time, the power that opposes God's plan will be destroyed before the actual exodus takes place. The Globalists will not pull off their gambit; they will not reach their ultimate goal. This is the end of the road for them.

So, the worldwide event that will precede the actual exodus 2.0 is the complete destruction of the Globalist One-World-Order. Just like the event that preceded Moses' exodus 1.0 was the complete destruction of Egyptian kingdom and power.

At that time, Jesus will identify every descendant of Jacob in ever country of the world. He will extricate them from their ambient societies. Judge them there in front of us all. He will cull out and destroy those who reject Him (Jesus is the only covenant). This culling—as we will propose later—might be at the heart of the destruction of the fourth empire. And with great fanfare, witnessed by everyone in the world, Jesus will move the blessed remnant into Israel. The rest of the events will follow as planned.

The One-World-Order, an empire divided

Let's go back to the nature of the fourth empire and fill in some more blanks. Besides the inherent weakness of money as a cohesive agent, the Globalist One-World-Order is a divided empire for the following realities:

1. As explained above, the feet—the bases—are terminally compromised. Then, to make things impossible spiritually:

true followers of Jesus will never mix, join, nor embrace this Globalists' empire.

1. The elites' intention was never to unite, but to gain absolute power over the lives and physical habitat of the masses. So they divide to conquer and enslave; they have to divide everyone so that no group can question or oppose their power—and no two groups may unite. They brutalize the masses because they want to have absolute control over the minds of the downtrodden. So, by process, this is a divided empire. (Their patsies in our midst are as ruthless as their overlords: they do not allow for anything to threaten their privileges and benefits.)

2. This cabal is addicted to killing people (after all, man is made in God's image, a concept they reject and abhor: they hate people). They have fomented wars incessantly, financing both sides of every conflict. Later, they sat in the courts of the nations and controlled the post-conflict settlements to their advantage, further enslaving the suffering people. They brought back the ancient, brutal malevolence of abortion and insist on imposing its use. The One-World-Government/New-World-Order can only attract those it bribes; but it naturally repulses its victims—it is divided.

3. The core of this cabal hates its own lackeys. Indeed, one feels only contempt and hatred for the ones he suborns, the ones he bribes. Bribing reinforces superiority. Over the years we have witnessed how this cabal eliminates the ones who have worn out their paid usefulness.

4. This cabal undermines good government, split the natural family nucleus, erodes the values of regional cohesions... It divides, divides and divides.

5. This One-World-Government elite works against the very

people it controls. It plans and pursues depopulation; not the caring husbanding and the natural growth of the population—this is hardly a uniting agenda.

6.   Even though it fostered coalitions of states like the United Nations, the European Union, universal agencies like the WHO, the WEF, UNICEF...the members of these and their many distinct peoples do not hold together. These organizations are artificial so they do not have a natural cohesion of the people they aim to rule. They have yet to achieve any benefit at all for the people they are supposed to serve. To wit: the record of UN interventions is awful, its corruption and violence are rampant. It exists simply to disarm and pressure independent states to surrender their control and armed services to this foreign, unelected and laterally unaccountable body. They are bottomless money pits that financially enslave humanity.

7.   And always, anywhere, this supra-national empire targets the true followers of Jesus. Sadly, they have scored some seditious victories in many of our churches as well. Yet, in spite of the woeful corruption and decay of some of the churches, the true faithful stand apart: they are divided from the "slag"; but not by it.

And finally, there is a stark division in the "empire" of this Elite's New-World-Order. The Elite considers itself to be the only proprietor of wisdom and knowledge. They have decreed that all the resources of earth belong to them. They have given themselves the privilege of deciding the future for all and creation.

They control the manipulations of capital and of the fiat moneys. They assert a self-given right to dictate and impose their agenda on the rest of the population—and any means justifies this end. They champion the "us" versus "them" concept—a dividing process.

They accept no established moral control over themselves; but they develop and impose their own self-serving, ever-changing morality on everyone else. They attempt to drown the reality of their completely parasitic existence with endless empty narratives and threats. They produce nothing; they are life-sucking parasites, every one of them... and they make mistakes upon mistakes. They are neither good nor gifted at running the world.

The masses are not the only targets and victims of their enslavement; the cabal compromises its own patsies and then impose on them the tyranny of blackmail. It is mercilessly divisive within its own ranks.

Today, the productive folks at large are beginning to understand that their personal worth is independent from the imposed uni-line of thoughts. The people who can produce and provide are slowly waking up to the fact that they could very well live and function outside the imposed system. Should the fourth empire framework be taken out; the producers would go on. So, when it does happen; the producers will shake off all the artificial control and go on! At least, this is the way it looks to me; what do you think?

Some courageous producers realizing their intrinsic value, begin to calculate the cost of this Globalist life-sucking, parasitic cancer on their livelihood, on their values and on their future and that of their children. They are moving away or resisting the over-reach of the Elite. They are getting ready to walk free. Just when the elite need the joining of the masses, their divisive policies have made this impossible—in the end: they cannot help themselves from failing!

This fourth empire is indeed a divided kingdom. The feet of iron mixed with clay are exhibiting their weakness, showing the cracks... And soon, the Rock will strike. Having dealt with division; let us now consider the destructive function of this empire.

The One-World-Order, the destroying empire

A judgment about any matter must rest on established and verified facts. Judging the fourth empire should be based on the same principle. How destructive has the fourth empire been? Does it fulfill the prophecy? Like iron, this globalist cabal is *strong as iron—for iron shatters and breaks everything—and just as iron smashes everything, so will it shatter and crush all the others*. Has it been the case? Yes, it has.

1. The cabal's New-World-Order/One-World-Government has been the deadliest empire of all times, through an unending series of wars and revolutions, it has managed the killing of hundreds of millions of people on all continents... and continues to do so. Recently they have whipped our uninformed citizenry and non-savvy leaders into a frenzy for war in a country and region that have absolutely no direct implication for us... yet, we are financing the killing machine and send stockpiles of modern killing equipment. It only benefits our military industrial complex and its overlords.

1. At a time when world agriculture produces a surplus of foodstuff, this cabal of over-rulers has engineered and carried out mass famines on several continents, killing hundreds of million more. This is not the place to document some of these engineered mass famines; but you can do some easy research on the subject.

2. Through deceiving medical practices and "health" dictates over the last century, this cabal has compromised the lives of many millions and as we begin to see now, they are engineering the progressive decline and death of many. The practice of medicine is now imposed from top-down; it has become a corporate structure. It has abandoned the practices of healing. Patients are potential profit centers. Have you

noticed that the first thing the front offices at your doctor's do, when you check in, is to make sure you can pay? When they call you to pre-register you; the only data they ask about is your insurances and your ability to pay. You must enter the cash sluice before your care can be considered. (I am not referring to emergency care here.)

3. This empire destroys the fiber of traditional, historical societies. The One-World-Government/New-World-Order elites carve God out of His creation, breaking the anchor of mental and spiritual sanity of the many. They deny the image of God in man. They promote the concept that the individual should come up with his own image; and they enforce the acceptance thereof on everybody else. They pound relentlessly on the divine order of the man-and-wife union that is the enduring bedrock of society. They are even working assiduously at making men into women and vice versa, knowing very well that the wrecking of the physical person wreck the inside as well—making the deluded desperately dependent upon the manipulators' promised "solutions". Every one of these issues is destructive.

Yet, the Globalist cabal is nervous: For all its frantic activities and formidable presence, the hold of this elite's empire remains tenuous because its only basic weapon is money. Its only foundation is the systematic corruption of the greedy and of the parasites. Yet, for all its corruptive capacity, money is the weakest of all controls. So, they use wars to hide this weakness, famines to deflect the concerns, diseases to blind the masses with fear, emotionally amplified false flags to distract... and the masses are constantly being played. It is a empire of lies.

Never again

We are told that Jesus (*the stone*) will set up a kingdom whose power and authority will never be given to such a human king or human supra-national system.

The One-World-Government/New-World-Order empire and all its trappings will be destroyed. Per Daniel's text, it will be pulverized by Jesus. And daft would be anyone who discounts what God so clearly predicted long ago.

The Globalists' One-World-Government/New-World-Order will be pounded so fine that nothing tangible at all will come out of God's mortar when He sets his crushing pestle aside. All the politicians who have treacherously attached their selfish ambitions and fortunes to this empire will be left with nothing at all... and many, may lose their lives. It will be the same for the judges, and for the many corrupt implants in all the government offices. It will be the same for the press, the academia, the entertainment industry, for the controlling agencies, for those in the military who have sold out themselves to it, for the military industrial complex, for some of the churches and their leaders. The shock on all of us will be massive. Many will realize the full meaning of Jesus' teaching: *You cannot serve both God and money...*

Peter said: *It is important for you to understand what will happen in the last days.* We begin to see the wisdom in this admonition. Indeed, the shock will be massive, but the believer should not be thrown off-balance or lose hope. We should foreknow it, expect it, welcome it and glorify God about it. And in this way, we will be able to help others. If we bury our heads in the sand today, we will have only ourselves to blame when the shockwaves destabilize us.

The guilty men and women of the fourth empire will not face an ineffectual and toothless human justice; they will experience God's awesome and complete judgment—no plea bargaining, no false witnesses, no bought juries and no cheap emotional tears. God will be the judge and the enforcer. Actually, God's action goes further than the destruction of this fourth empire; it will be so total as to remove all traces, influences and identities of all four of the supra-national empires (*Not a trace of them could be found*). The fourth empire has borrowed and developed many traits from the others and all that will vanish. There will never be another human supra-national empire (*The stone... will fill the whole earth*).

And this is where Daniel's prophecy links up with outstanding prophecies for the Hebrew people. After Jesus pulverizes the Globalists construct and smashes its actors in every country <u>including</u> in the State of Israel, and immediately takes His Hebrew people to the land He gave them, they will never be subject to another human ruler. Ezekiel 20:21 – 24 promises: *I will gather the people of Israel from among the nations. I will bring them home to their own land from the places where they have been scattered... I will unify them into one nation on the mountains of Israel. One king will rule them all; no longer will they be divided into two nations or into two kingdoms... My servant David will be their king, and they will have only one shepherd. They will obey my regulations and be careful to keep my decrees.*

King David of antiquity does not come back to reign; it is Jesus, the direct descendant of David, the Lion of Judah, who will be that king. So, from the time Jesus moves His Hebrew people into the land—very shortly after destroying the fourth empire—Jesus permanently rules in that land and over these people. (His presence will not be physical at this time; not like it will be during the 1,000 year reign.)

If Jesus rules in one land, on this small planet called earth; won't He rule everywhere else too as Daniel tells us? Is this planet big enough for competing and antipathetic rulers to coexist with Jesus? Daniel 2 is clear: the *stone* will fill the earth—period. No other supra-national will ever develop.

> <u>Note</u>: We are not talking about absence of sin here; just the absence of competing world orders.

To me, it makes sense that after eliminating all traces of every supra-national empire that had ever existed, and as He rules in one land, Jesus will also be the only supra-national power in the Gentile world—just as Daniel 2 tells us. And time will be short from there on; the other events will follow apace.

Do other prophets agree with Daniel 2? Yes, for example, Isaiah 47 confirms the divine action that ends the empire *à la* Babylon:

1 "Come Babylon, unconquered one, sit in the dust. For your days of glory, pomp, and honor have ended. O daughter of Babylonia, never again will you be the lovely princess, tender and delicate. 2 Take heavy millstones and grind flour. Remove your veil, and strip off your robe. Expose yourself to public view. 3 You will be naked and burdened with shame. I will take vengeance against and will not negotiate."

4 Our Redeemer, whose name is the Lord of Heaven's Armies, is the Holy One of Israel.

5 "O beautiful Babylon, sit now in darkness and silence. Never again will you be known as the queen of kingdoms. 6 For I was angry with my chosen people and punished them by letting them fall into your hands. But you, Babylon, showed them no mercy. You oppressed even the elderly. 7 You thought, 'I will reign forever as queen of the world!' You did not care at all about my people or think about the consequences of your actions.

8 "You are a pleasure-crazy kingdom, living at ease and feeling secure, bragging as if you were the greatest in the world! You say, 'I am self-sufficient and not accountable to anyone! I will never be a widow *or lose my children.' **9** Well, both these things will come upon you in a moment: widowhood and the loss of your children. Yes, these calamities will come upon you, despite all your witchcraft and magic.*

*__10__ "You felt secure in your wickedness. 'No one sees me,' you said. Your 'wisdom' and 'knowledge' have caused you to turn away from me and claim, 'I am self-sufficient and not accountable to anyone!' **11** So disaster will overtake you suddenly, and you won't be able to charm it away. Calamity will fall upon you, and you won't be able to buy your way out. A catastrophe will strike you suddenly, one for which you are not prepared.*

*__12__ "Call out the demon hordes you have worshiped all these years! Ask them to help you strike terror into the hearts of people once again. **13** You have more than enough advisers, astrologers, and stargazers. Let them stand up and save you from what the future holds. **14** But they are like straw burning in a fire; they cannot save themselves from the flame. You will get no help from them at all; their hearth is no place to sit for warmth. **15** And all your friends, those with whom you've done business since childhood, will go their own ways, turning a deaf ear to your cries.* (Isiah 47:1 – 15 NLT)

And that is that.

Note the many qualifiers that identify our fourth empire. And note the congruity with Daniel 2: *Calamity will fall upon you, and you won't be able to buy your way out. A catastrophe will strike you suddenly, one for which you are not prepared.*

Israel

The land of Israel versus the state of Israel

Supporting texts for this section can also be found in Hosea chapters 10,11,12; Ezekiel chapters 20, 28 and 38; Isaiah 11, 52 (plus a confirming image in Isaiah 8:11 – 15).

Let us begin with Isaiah 8:11 – 15 NCV which foretells of the time of testing for the Hebrews—the process Ezekiel will define precisely. These verses do not seem germane to the time of Isaiah or the few centuries that followed. The message seems to be projecting much further into the future.

God spoke clearly to Isaiah: *People are saying that others make plans against them, but you should not believe them. Do not be afraid of what they fear; do not dread those things. But remember that the LORD All-powerful is holy. He is the one you should fear; He is the one you should dread. Then He will be a place of safety for you. But for the two families of Israel, He will be a stone that causes people to stumble, like a rock that makes them fall. He will be like a trap for the people of Jerusalem, and will catch them in His trap. Many people will fall over this rock. They will fall and be broken; they will be trapped and caught.*

In these short few verses, God identifies our time: Today, we are indeed awash with a vast current of conspiratorial stories and rumors, we see alarming developments. There are rumors of manipulations of humanity into a degraded species, torn from its maker's composition, rumors of cataclysmic population decimations, rumors of complete, inescapable controls of every aspect of life and of thought... We are indeed at the time when soon the rock will cause Isaiah's people to stumble, to fall, to be broken.

And this is the time when the "rock" (same rock as Daniel 2's) will be used by God to sift the righteous Hebrews from the damnable Hebrews. This is the time of testing for the Hebrews. And as God foresees, many Hebrews will be eliminated upon this confrontation with the "rock". (For the Gentiles the time of testing, as per Revelation, will be the three and one-half years of what is commonly, but erroneously, called "the tribulations".)

When we read the texts about the exodus 2.0, we are told that this exodus will follow the prototype given in Moses' time. We are also told that in each country where they reside, God will identify every Hebrew descendant—the Jews (tribes of Judah and Benjamin) plus the ten northern tribes of Israel. In each land, He will call them out of the local, general population, and while in the no-man's land of society there, He will judge them. Ezekiel 20:34 and 37 says: ... *I will raise my powerful arm and punish you. I will show my anger against you... I will judge you guilty and punish you according to the agreement* [Jesus is the only agreement, the only covenant]. They will be judged and punished according to the new covenant: Jesus—the Jesus they have rejected all along.

> Note: The Hebrews who have already come to Jesus have nothing to fear from this process. Those who at that time surrender to Jesus will be spared.

The charge of the judgement is whether or not a person will accept God's eternal covenant. The covenant made in Moses' time was fulfilled by Jesus; so, the only covenant of God since Calvary is Jesus. He will publicly destroy the Hebrews who refuse Him now—He will kill them. The others, He will majestically usher them out of all their countries with great pomp and awesome power. He will go before them and behind them. And, on their phones, tablets or other screens, everyone throughout the world will see Jesus do this in their respective country—live and in real time.

As part of the destruction of the fourth empire, God (Jesus) will do in the State of Israel what He will do to the Hebrews in all the other countries: He will make the people pass under His rod regarding the everlasting covenant. See Ezekiel 20:38; *I will remove them from your homeland.* (Which implies that this particular group of Hebrews were already in Israel to begin with.) So, in the State of Israel, God/Jesus will obliterate every Jew who turns down His eternal covenant—Jesus. So, the same culling of the Hebrews that we will witness in our countries will concurrently take place in the State of Israel. The ERV translation rendered Ezekiel 20:37 – 38 as follows: "*I will judge you guilty and punish you according to the agreement. I will remove all those who turned against Me and sinned against Me. I will remove them from your homeland. They will never again come to the land of Israel. Then you will know that I am the LORD.*"

God will identify His ancient people

> <u>Note</u>: When I refer to Jews, I usually refer to the tribes of Judah and Benjamin. The two tribes that remained identifiable after the Northern ten tribes were driven to exile, when they spread out into the world and were lost in history. The twelve tribes together are the descendants of Jacob: the Hebrews. All Hebrews are God's ancient people and all will benefit from His loving dispensations.

Today, there does not seem to exist any connective records that would tie a person to a Hebraic true lineage to Jacob; the last reliable records were destroyed almost 2,000 years ago when the temple of Jerusalem was razed. It is God who, in our time, will identify all the descendants of Jacob (both the Jews and the rest of the ten tribes). Ezekiel 37 gives us this divine process. These descendants of Jacob have lost their identity (they are the dry bones of Ezekiel 37); they are not humanly identifiable: How could one connect these bones to their ancestor's identity? The line of continuity has been lost somewhere in time.

So, by now, as far as human knowledge goes, people cannot be verifiably identified as God's ancient people—as bonafide Hebrews. Jacob's descendants are not differentiable from others. No one but God knows who they are—even though today, millions identify as Jewish; we won't know until God reveals those who are.

It is God who will give them back their identity—He identifies them from among the populations of the world. He knows who everyone is. This is what the vision of the valley of the dry bones tells us.

As described above, having identified them, God will extricate them from the society of Gentile populations of the world (yes, even in the State of Israel). And then, in plain sight of the whole world, God will judge these legitimate descendants of Jacob on the basis of His covenant (Jesus). Jesus will publicly destroy the Hebrews who reject Him as Messiah and lead to Israel those who embrace Him as Messiah.

> <u>Note</u>: This divine process of identification did not happen for the creation of the State of Israel in 1948. It is yet to be realized, but for the sake of simplicity, I will continue to refer to those who claim Jewishness as Jews. Whether or not they will ultimately be proven to be so.

Did exodus 2.0 begin in 1948?

However much we Christians may yearn to see the blessed exodus take place; exodus 2.0 was not set in motion in 1948. None of the irreducible attributes of exodus 2.0—as given by the prophets—were present.

Ezekiel is very straight forward: *This is what the Lord God says: **I** will gather the people of Israel from the nations where they are scattered. **I** will show my holiness when the nations see what I do for my people. Then they will live in their own land—**the land I gave** to my servant Jacob. **They will live safely** in the land and will build houses and plant vineyards. They will live in safety **after I have punished all the nations around who hate them. Then they will know that I am the Lord their God*** (28:25 – 26 NCV, emphasis mine).

God will not share the glory nor the credit for and around exodus 2.0: He will carry it out and will get all the credit. And every living Hebrew will know that Jesus is the Lord their God. God did not need the British nor the United Nations to accomplish this; they were not His helpers—they have been His usurpers. The Balfour resolution, the documents that preceded the creation of the State of Israel, the conundrums that accompanied its dismal execution have never been of God. No human political pretender will "grant" a geographical place to God's ancient people in the land He specifically gave them; how pretentious! Idolatrous, human hubris engineered the State of Israel. Christians should have been wise to this.

So, let us look at why the State of Israel is not the Israel God will establish in the exodus of our time.

- In and around 1948, God did not specifically identify all the descendants of Jacob—including the "lost" ten tribes.

- In and around the 1948 creation of the State of Israel, the rebellious Hebrews were not judged and destroyed by God in all the countries where they live before Jesus moved the rest, who would have embraced the covenant (Jesus), into Israel.

• The move into the land of Israel did not happen all at once, from everywhere in the world as prophesied.

• And the majority of the Hebrew people still live outside the state of Israel. A fact that does not mesh with the second exodus—the exodus will be total. Not a single living Hebrew will be left behind (Ezekiel 39:28).

• The divinely led exodus will happen <u>simultaneously</u> everywhere, <u>from every country</u>. It did not happen in 1948 or since.

• No human politics, and no army will be involved. That did not happen.

• Undisturbed peace did not follow the creation of the State of Israel; the opposite happened: relentless conflicts have ruled life there. One could even say that the human creation of the State of Israel was done is such a way that it insured endless strife and wars.

• And, all the Hebrews who moved to Israel have certainly not come to Jesus... (neither before nor since).

• God has not "punished all the nations around them who hate them"; this is what God will accomplish through the conflict of Gog and Magog.

• For the true final exodus, God will reunite the twelve tribes of Israel <u>before</u> He brings them into the promise land (Ezekiel 37). This non-negotiable fact did not happen. In fact, no one in Israel ever mentioned the ten northern tribes to me. Even more revealing, the shameless moochers—Jewish Christians of Israel—who incessantly solicit American Christians for donations for their various "ministries", never mention the fact that the ten tribes are neither identified nor present in today's State of Israel. Why? Simply because bringing this fact to light would expose the parody that is today's State of Israel. (And probably cut off their grifting funding.)

• Plus, through the current process, the nations have not known that YHWH/Jesus is LORD and that He is the Holy One in Israel (Ezekiel 39:7). This is one of God's own purposes.

The three prophetic standards to evaluate the State of Israel' legitimacy

Ezekiel 37 gives us three defining standards by which we can judge the current State of Israel. God said to Ezekiel: *The people of Israel say "our bones have dried up; our hope is gone. We have been completely destroyed..."* Indeed, the ten tribes of Israel are buried in the cemetery of history—under the dust of oblivion—and also many actual descendants of Judah and Benjamin remain unidentified. We and they can't say whether or not they are from the Hebrew tribes. Am I, or are you, a descendant of one of the 12 tribes?

Today, only God knows and he addresses this. *So speak to them for Me. Tell them this is what the Lord GOD says: "My people, I will open your graves and bring you out of them! Then I will bring you to the land of Israel... My people, I will open your graves and bring you up out of your graves, and then you will know that I am the LORD..."* Having thus identified all the Hebrews, not just the Jews, but all the descendants of Jacob, God continues: *I will put my spirit in you and you will come to life again.* (Jesus is the life, the life more abundantly. This will happen to every one who accept the covenant of Jesus as Messiah. God says He will judge them according to the covenant. The only covenant is Jesus.)

Then I will lead you back to your own land. Then you will know that I am the LORD. You will know that I said this and that I made it happen. The text is clear: the second exodus toward the land of Israel will only begin after the first process is completed. This absolutely did not happen for 1948—and it has yet to happen today.

The second standard we are given is also found in the rest of the 37th chapter of Ezekiel: It is the permanent reunion of all the twelve tribes of Israel as one people, forever. They are reunited before the God-led exodus 2.0 begins! This has not happened at all.

The third standard is this: From the time they are identified then have passed under the rod (of their acceptance or refusal of the covenant: Jesus), they will be led by their king—Jesus, the heir (and Lord) of David. Jesus will be their only leader—permanently. This obviously did not happen then, and it has yet to take place. Jesus certainly does not reign in Israel today and He is not the Lord of the majority of the Jewish population there.

The reality of the State of Israel

Accordingly, there are solid arguments in favor of the current State of Israel and Zionism being crafty decoys from the enemy; let's look into this.

The modern State of Israel is a strange construct. It is completely modeled on the secular national organization of the countries of the world; it does not reflect a land given by YHWH. Its charters were given (imposed?) to it by men and by the political means of men. It fits perfectly into the Globalists One-World-Government model because the very leaders of this empire were the movers and pushers of the Zionist movement and the creation of this reality of false hope.

From the news I follow and from personal experience the few times my work took me to Israel, I say that the country is a mess. Very few of its citizens follow Messiah. Some of the people I dealt with are atheists—and proud to be. Some are very corrupt... From what I have observed, morality is absent at all levels. And, the Globalist One-World-Government/One-World-Order runs the State of Israel and all its functionalities. What I did not see while in Israel was Jesus being taught, promoted and glorified as the Jewish Messiah. From what I understand, now and again, there are even laws proposed against proselytizing in Israel. Imagine that: some Jewish people in Israel want to enact a law against the proselytizing of the very Messianic covenant upon which all the Hebrews will be judged for exodus 2.0! If this last item is not a powerful argument against 1948 being exodus 2.0; I can't think of what is!

Israel today is not the land that follows the God of Heaven and Earth through Jesus. It is a misguided human workaround to God's glorious plan. The current state of Israel is a diabolical decoy. Armed conflicts predictably succeed one another in that country, strife define its social life. (It is exactly the type of behaviors the fourth empire strives on.) When God enacts His plan, there will be peace in that land (even Gog and Magog will not require any military involvement from the Hebrews).

The consequences of the State of Israel

As a decoy, the State of Israel effectively derailed well meaning Christians everywhere from the reality of the scriptures. In their desire to bless the Israelites, they overlooked the specificity of the prophecies. A well-meaning, but scripturally wrong pastor recently said: exodus 2.0

was in 1948... although he was hard-pressed to justify the constant state of war since then... Let's be real: Either the 1948 State of Israel is exodus 2.0 and peace has reigned since then, or it isn't... and wars have been waged.

The Zionist State of Israel has also derailed well meaning Jews everywhere by providing a deceptive focus about their return to their land without first coming to their Messiah Jesus. It encourages them to continue on their deadly Pharisaic/Talmudic mindset that has kept so many from coming to Jesus' light and life in the last two millennia.

There are no by-passes; the prophecies clearly demand a chronology: first, all the world Hebrews will be identified, then separated out of the local populations. Then, they will be judged on the basis of God's covenant (Jesus) and only then, Jesus will lead the covenant embracers into their God-given land. Jesus is the only door by which every Jew (and Hebrew) must pass to get transferred to their given land. For the Jewish people, the current decoy is a cruel proposition; it pitilessly abuses their deep, heartfelt yearning. It prevents them from making the necessary about-face on their religious stand about Jesus. It is a deadly diversion.

There is one thing I have noticed though: the One-World-Government/New-World-Order is very much present in the State of Israel. The Globalist elite cabal is very active and rooted in the system. Their tenets are the reality of life there. I believe this fact to be significant. One of the foremost expositor of the One-World-Order is Mr. Hariri, a Jew living in Israel. What it says to me is that, at this moment, the State of Israel is just like any other country. It is not the blessed land of the Hebrews; it is the State of Israel where some Hebrews live—most of them rebellious.

The State of Israel has been sustained by massive influx of funds from the Globalist Deep State of many countries—instead of being divinely ushered, blessed and kept by God. It has been artificially and parasitically propped up financially, politically and militarily. It has taxed the well-meaning Gentile Christians everywhere. It has not been smiled on by God in the way Isaiah, Ezekiel and the others waxed lyrically. I am fully aware of the jubilant rhetoric of sabra Messianic Jews who read everything through an expectant and optimistic lens, touting the State of Israel as the de facto exodus 2.0. "Hopium" only changes emotions; not facts. I too had been blinded to this reality in my fervor to support the cause of my God's ancient people. But, eventually, I had to reckon with the expressed prophetic messages.

The current State of Israel is not set up to serve YHWH. It does not exist to magnify Him and especially not Jesus. When God finally returns the Hebrews to the <u>land</u> of Israel; they will all serve Him, magnify Him and rejoice in Him, in and through Jesus. God will then impose and maintain His divine peace there for all the Hebrews.

Upon reflection, it looks to me that the State of Israel is a sinful, evil construct. That land is special; it is meant to be set apart. It was never meant to mimic the rest of the countries—especially not the fourth empire! It is due for a serious cleansing. God set the Hebrews apart; He does not intend them to dovetail neatly into an existing and overtly anti-God system.

Drawing the conclusions

So what happened? Very simply: The enemy snuck in a decoy. The Satanic cabal set up, sponsored and have been running a false exodus 2.0. We Christians fell for the decoy. And it sure threw a monkey wrench in the Christian circles and it divided the Hebrews everywhere, giving them false hope.

The Christians ecstatically wishing to see prophecy fulfilled in their time overlooked the details, they passed over the facts and fudged God's word. The evil scheme worked. It worked against its intended targets: Christians and Hebrews. The Christians fell for it and once more lost their scriptural moorings. The Hebrews' heart desire soared on false hopes. And war followed war.

Indeed, the scheme worked for the Satanic cabal: it created permanent conflicts, misery and turned people away from the truth. It impoverished the supporting countries by draining their funds to sustain this parasitic decoy. We Christians failed to be wise about this; we should have demanded that every item of coordinated scriptures be validated and checked before being emotionally moved. We certainly have not acted in a Berean fashion about this at all—we acted more like Pavlovian dogs.

Had the Christians held the scriptural line; so many heartaches, so much mourning, so much false hopes could have been avoided. As it stands, though, every few years we are whipped up into a frenzy of indignation, of "righteous anger" and into monetary support to counteract a new conflict. Even as I write these words (2023), a new iteration of the same scheme has just begun and we Christians are being washed overboard by real and fabricated media and we are sounding the war drums in favor of Israel... After all, aren't we supposed to be staunch supporters of, allies to the Hebrews and Israel?... Except that this is not the Israel of prophecies.

And, periodically, the demand for a "two state solution" ramps up anew. Polemic and furor burn hot about it. I used to get my knickers in a twist about it. No, no, I would say along with most Christians I know: Israel is given to the Hebrews by God. No one can divide it... Except, it is not the Israel of Exodus 2.0. This is the decoy, the Globalists' State of Israel; so: let them divide it. Let them do whatever they want with it:

in the end, God will give the whole Land of Israel to the true Hebrews and nobody, but nobody, will ever be able to contest any part of it. Every single soldier marching against God's Israel at the battle of Gog and Magog will pay the ultimate price at the hand of God and the countries they represent will never consider going against the Hebrews, ever again.

Exodus 2.0 will happen; and it will happen exactly as God promised it, fulfilling every iota of the ancient prophetic scriptures. And it will happen very soon.

For all the reasons expanded above, the same processes of Daniel 2 and of the culling of the Hebrews people everywhere will also take place inside the State of Israel—a country just like all the others.

As we have proposed above, before Jesus brings His Hebrew people out of the countries of the world and into the land of Israel, He will destroy our fourth empire—the supra-national empire of the Globalists. Therefore, we can expect that He will carry out the destruction of the same Globalist Empire in the State of Israel as well; a state that is no different from any other human, secular organization. A state that is special today only by its geography.

As part of the process introducing exodus 2.0 God will obliterate the fourth empire that currently rules in the State of Israel. There will not even be a trace of it left. Having done this, Jesus, the stone, will also grow to fill the power vacuum within the entire land of Israel—just as He will do everywhere else in the world.

As we have already covered above in the text, God (Jesus) will do in Israel to the Jews and Hebrews living there what He will do to the Hebrews in all the other countries: He will make the people pass under His rod regarding the everlasting covenant. So, in the State of Israel, God/Jesus will obliterate every Jew who turns down His eternal covenant—Jesus. So, the same culling of the Hebrews that we will witness in our countries will concurrently take place in the State of Israel (Ezekiel 20:37 – 38).

In my opinion, once this triage and purge is done, the LAND of Israel (as opposed to the State of Israel) will be ready to receive the Hebrew expats from every other country. As Ezekiel promises: None will be left behind. And the Hebrews already there, having embraced God's Messianic covenant, will be filled with joy.

As best as I can understand, there never was a secular State of Israel in God's economy. The Land of Israel was always a theocracy, a land divinely provided for the descendants of Jacob. A people sustained by their God and not an artificial, parasitic construct that syphons the funds and economies of well meaning—but gullible—Christians abroad.

And there too, it is Jesus who will personally be the Head and His rule will be the only rule. "*And give them this message from the Sovereign Lord: I will gather the people of Israel from among the nations. I will bring them home to their own land from the places where they have been scattered. I will unify them into one nation on the mountains of Israel. One king will rule them all; no longer will they be divided into two nations or into two kingdoms. They will never again pollute themselves with their idols and vile images and rebellion, for I will save them from their sinful apostasy. I will cleanse them. Then they will truly be my people, and I will be their God. My servant David will be their king, and they will have only one shepherd. They will obey my regulations and be careful to keep my decrees*" (Ezekiel 37:21 – 24)

The stone not cut by human hands that will grow to fill the whole world, will also fill the land of Israel: *My servant David will be their king.* This is Jesus, of whom David was only a human foreshadow.

The Jews and the new world order

The Jewish enigma

Who is Jewish? And just as importantly: What has been the development path of the Pharisaic/Talmudic religious sect over the centuries? Two different sets of questions can be raised about this, but they are facets of the same greater whole.

Do we know who is Jew/Hebrew? Do we even know if we, ourselves are? And, do the true descendants of Jacob know who they are? Maybe, maybe not; some historical factors have to be considered.

And, wouldn't the logical extension of the anti-Jesus aim of the Pharisaic/Talmudic sect eventually target the whole of humanity? Indeed, this Satanic sect diverted the majority of the Jews away from Jesus and kept them away from Him. Wouldn't their hatred of God's Savior push them to do the same for the rest of humanity? Isn't this precisely their master Satan's ambition? The answer to those questions is: Yes, of course. Eventually the Pharisaic/Talmudic elite would not limit their reach to the "Jews". Let us pick up the thread from its inception.

As far as I can find out, within a couple of centuries prior to Jesus' first coming, Satan promoted a new Hebraic sect: the Pharisees. They were merciless and aggressive, they aimed to control every aspect of Jewish life. Disobeying their dictates brought shunning at best, and a death sentence at worst. They became dominant and they highjacked the Jewish faith and they shunted the people away from the forgiveness of sin through Jesus—which was the sect's true purpose: To separate God's chosen people from Him. The Pharisees rejected Jesus and made sure the people did too. They ostracized and persecuted the Jews who followed and embraced Jesus. People feared them.

The Pharisees completely subverted the ancient faith, downplayed the written Torah while they inserted a wholly made-up "oral tradition texts": the Talmud which they have used assiduously to mislead the people away from Jesus as Messiah. They did away with the priests and priesthood, they set up the rabbinical order and promoted the Talmud. This Talmudic sect has been the only form of "Judaism" since then. The Judaism of Moses' Torah had led directly to Jesus but Talmudic Judaism leads away from Jesus.

The Jews, having rejected Jesus were exiled to the four corners of the world by the Romans. They took with them their divergent faith.

These two facts—the absence of means to identify real Jews and the Pharisaic/Talmudic Judaism as the only form of Judaism—affect our perception today. First is the lack of records. The genealogical records of the ten northern tribes seem to have disappeared with their exile twenty-five centuries ago—so we and they don't know who they are. And the records of the two remaining tribes which were kept in the temple might have been destroyed or lost when the Romans destroyed the temple. So, who are the descendants of the Israelites of antiquity today? I am not sure we can assess this positively.

Second: Most of the Jews that the Romans scattered abroad carried on the non-scriptural Talmudic religion. (The Mosaic Judaism having found its fulfillment in Jesus naturally disappeared—as it was meant to.) The Pharisees tricked every Jew to think that their Talmudic heresy was in fact true Judaism. And the switch stuck.

Third: Gentiles who converted to the "Jewish" faith since the Roman exile have in fact embraced the Pharisaic Talmudic false religion. And having embraced the religion, they eventually claimed to be Jewish—to affirm their legitimacy. With the passage of time and generations, their own lore evolved and today's their descendants are persuaded that they are—and have always been—Jewish.

Through the centuries, these factors have created a confusing situation: Are all the people who claim to be Jewish actually descendants of Jacob? Or are many of them simply Gentile converts to the Talmudic sect with no direct ascendance to Jacob? I am not qualify to draw the line on this, and I am not convinced anybody can. The "legacy Jews" and the Gentiles who attached themselves to Talmudic Judaism do not follow the God of the Bible. They confess the god of the Pharisees—the god without Jesus. This in no way ties them to Moses.

We can rest on the fact that at exodus 2.0 God will extract the true Hebrews from the Gentile populations amongst which they live. Even where no human clues exist visibly, God knows who His chosen people are (see the dry bones, Ezekiel 37). Many true Hebrews today do not know they are Jews. (Probably quite many of them are already follower of Messiah Jesus.) As for those who claim to be Jewish; God knows those whose blood is Jacob's and those whose roots are elsewhere.

Jesus made it clear that there was nothing good with the Pharisees' movement, He made sure we understood that Satan is their master. When Paul says that he was the worst sinner; he was right: by being a devoted, zealot Pharisee, he was indeed deeply sinful. Viz.: When Jesus got his attention, Paul was on his way to persecute, kill and abduct people whose only "sin" was to have come to Jesus—God's true Savior! Before his conversion, Paul was a true Talmudic heretic.

The elite core of the Globalist cabal today who claim Hebraic root and embrace the Pharisaic Talmudic faith still serve the same master—and today, they do not even hide their allegiance to the prince of darkness. These and their followers are the ones who God will completely destroy (Jeremiah 30:11). As far as the true descendants of Jacob, God will judge them on the basis of the new covenant and He will only destroy those who turn Him down.

God's actions will bring clarity

So, how does the divine action of Daniel 2 fit into this?

It does simply because the authorship and the leadership of the Globalists' New-World-Order has a "Jewish" element, at its core. And these particular descendants of Jacob—true or assumed—have devised and enforced the coercive "fourth empire" specifically meant to destroy the Messiah-based Christianity. They mean to eradicate all signs and witnesses of YHWH/Jesus as creator and God of all. And they aim to demean man—the apogee of God's creation. Whether true Hebrews or pretenders, they have diligently carried out the anti-Jesus Pharisaic's legacy.

Jesus clearly says that He is the light and the life. The Satanic sect that diverted God's chosen people from the light and from the life was bound to expand their quest and eventually attempt to subvert all of humanity in the entire world. And this is the New-World-Order. It took many centuries, but it is culminating just in time for the events of our time.

These descendants of Jacob—real or pretenders—have purposefully dethroned Jesus. Thus these individuals will, in no way, accept the lordship of the One they hate and despise. Therefore whether true Jews or Gentile pretenders, these will be killed divinely. So, true to scriptures, God will kill them in the foreign lands of their adoption as well as in Israel. So, we can conceive that a component of the action of the "stone, not cut by human hands" of Daniel 2 will be this specific destruction of the willfully wayward descendants of Jacob who conceived and developed this fourth empire? And the destruction of the compromised Gentiles who joined them will be the just collateral effect. Basically, God will clear the slate, then He will carry out His majestic exodus 2.0.

He will thus eliminate any false notion of religious righteousness; the only gambit for all humans then will be Jesus or not Jesus. He will crush and eliminate the Satanic Talmudic sect.

A divine reset: two birds with one "Rock"

It seems that God will achieve several resets in one action:

1. Destroy the fourth empire, thus freeing universal humanity from this cruel, insidious, controlling, murderous and destructive yoke.
2. Destroy the false "Judaism" religion. Thus He eliminates the false concept of Judeo-Christian standard we hear bandied about all the time. It is a concept that only existed because the Talmudic Judaism claimed a root in Mose's Torah. Moses' Judaism having been integrated fully in Jesus, in Christianity. There is no post-Jesus Judeo-Christian reality.
    Before Jesus, there was only Judaism, since Jesus, there is only Christianity. In God's eyes, there have never been Judaism <u>and</u> Christianity; only Christianity within which Moses' Judaism is fulfilled. The abhorrent Judeo-Christian concept that gave legitimacy to the Pharisaic/Talmudic sect and muzzled Christians goes away.

The actions of the Rock clear the way, and set up the parameters for the only remaining spiritual battle: the battle between the real gospel of the real Christ and the false gospel of the false christ.

The New-World-Order

Let's look into its history:

It seems to me that the Talmudic Jewish component of the fourth empire was the creator and architect of the Globalist

One-World-Government. From what I read, it was Meyer Rothschild who convoked the 12 heads of the leading illuminati sects to propose a hellish, complete, world hegemony system: the New-World-Order. Its organization was spearheaded by Adam Weishaupt (another "Jewish" character). As the scion of Talmudic Judaism, this evil empire was specifically founded to destroy Christianity and all the foundations of Godliness, and to kill the God of Heaven. Its clarion of revolutions, Karl Marx (whose real name was Mordecai) and his contemporary cohort were "Jewish".

According to my readings, we find the same Talmudic Jewish component in every destructive revolution this global cabal wrought on the diverse populations of the world. I have read that the leadership—and the relentless impulsion to destroy—of the French Revolution of 1789 – 93 had such a "Jewish" core. The Russian revolution of 1917 and the terrible destruction in its aftermath definitely had a radical "Jewish" component and leadership. The same scenario reproduced itself in the Hungarian revolution. From what I read, Jewish international bankers financed every one of these endeavors. So, from Karl Marx to Bela Kun, the radical and evil revolutionary cadre had a predominantly, self-claimed, Jewish component.

In pre-Jesus times, Pharisaic/Talmudic judaism was conceived to shunt the descendants of Jacob from their promised Messiah Jesus and to dethrone God. Its control of the Jewish population was extreme, rigid and ubiquitous. The people feared the Pharisees. In great part Pharisaic/Talmudic Judaism met its goals: only a minority of courageous Jews came to Jesus. Through the centuries and to the present, Pharisaic/Talmudic Judaism has maintained its hold of the "Jewish" population. It still strives to control every aspect of those people's lives. The goals of the Pharisaic sect were always universal because destroying Jesus and Christianity was always a universal in scope. It was just a matter of time before this sect would put in place the systems that would railroad all of humanity toward perdition and put in place systems of complete control and harsh, unforgiving consequences. And this is where we are in history.

It seems that the fourth empire is the human effort to establish the promised Hebrew reign—but without God, outside God, in spite of God and against God... Making it a thoroughly evil undertaking. However, this was always going to end in failure. The fourth empire was always headed for destruction—divine destruction. The universal millennial kingdom God promised the descendants of Jacob will be ushered by Jesus, after He deals with the time of trouble and sends the antichrist and the false prophet into Hell. It is Jesus who will rule that kingdom for one thousand years—not a self-serving cabal. Several chapters of history must still be written before that millennial kingdom begins.

Daniel 2 (and Isaiah 47:1 – 15) tells us precisely that it is God who will put an end to the fourth empire cabal, the text tells us exactly what God will do with them and it gives us the outcome. So, one can only ponder: Is it because there is a self-claimed Jewish core component in this fourth empire, that it is God Himself who will destroy it, and not man as for the other three empires? Christians and Gentiles are not given the judgment sword against God's ancient people: God reserves that right for Himself.

And: Is it because exodus 2.0 is in the offing that this evil empire will be dealt with at this time, as the necessary, timely, clearing of the spiritual field for the culling of His true ancient people? Can we conceive that having eliminated the Talmudic pretenders, God can then bring out the genuine descendants of Jacob: the anonymous and forgotten "dried bones" of Ezekiel 37? I tend to answer yes to the questions above. What do you think?

As written previously, we will all witness a swift succession of amazing divine events: The identifying then culling of the real descendants of Jacob, the majestic and divine transfer of the remainder descendants of Jacob to Israel, the opening up of the entire territory of the greater land of Israel to the Hebraic tribes and the seven year blissful hiatus in history when God will rejoice with His ancient people in Israel. Two considerations make it clear as to the timing and the process of the elimination of the evil fourth empire: it is biblically and logically coherent that our current evil empire and its consequences should be dealt with now, in our time, and, second, that God should be the effector. He has the divine right to deal with His people—real and pretenders... So He will.

In Nebuchadnezzar's empire, and by presumption in empires two and three, the Jewish people were victims or at least mere subjects. This current fourth empire appears different: It seems that the power elite is ubiquitously "Jewish" at the higher echelons and the rest of the peoples of the world—the "non-elite Hebrews" and the Gentiles—are the victims or at least mere subjects. The avowed goal of the cabal is to enslave everyone who is not of the tiny anti-Messiah Jewish elite.

Therefore, it is easy to conceive that God must destroy the pretenders, this Talmudic/Satanic Jewish cabal; thus removing the false before bringing out to the light the true Hebrew people. This clearing out of the field will help both the Gentiles and the Hebrews. Erasing the scriptural off-ramp that is the Pharisaic/Talmudic religion will clear the way for the great harvest: Scriptures will become unified and clear, there will not be a Jewish religion and a Christian religion, there will only be Christ—the unifier of scripture from creation to the end. (This is what the divine reality has been since Jesus.) And finally, all the real Hebrews Jesus spares will have come to Him.

<u>Note</u>: We also need to address a point that is skirted in all the discussions about the holocaust of the Nazi regimes around the second World War: Many of the international grand financiers who financed Hitler's regime and the war did not share in the decimation of their co-descendants of Jacob—real or assumed. None of the "Jewish" financiers ended in the death camps. None of them were targeted in the streets. They seemed inured to the pains and deaths of millions of their own "Jewish" brothers and sisters: those whose deaths and pains they were knowingly financing. These powerful, behind-the-scene obscene, Jewish/Talmudic sponsors of war and misery could have stopped the concentration camps and death camps even before WWII began by removing their funding! At any point during that awful war they could have stopped all of it by doing the same... Why didn't they? Who else, but them, could really and honestly be blamed? We blame Hitler and his Nazis (they deserve the blame) but we do not blame his enablers—who are even more guilty. These obscene Hebrew/Jewish/Talmudic individuals and their families walked away unpunished—and richer... The Rock will strike them.

The new testament connections to Daniel 2 with Jesus' confirmation

In Luke, there are two direct connections to Daniel 2. We find them in Luke 17:26 – 37 and Luke 20:13 – 19.

In Luke 17, Jesus talks to the Hebrews about the Hebrews in Samaria or in Jerusalem. This passage has nothing to do with the rapture, or the majestic coming down of Jesus to reign on earth for one thousand years.

The Pharisees ask: when will the Kingdom of God come? Meaning when will the royal Messiah, the new David come and establish his thousand year reign with us as the "übermenchen"? They had rejected the prophetic details that foretold a suffering and atoning Messiah. They wanted to jump directly to the "big" time. The time that would justify <u>them</u>.

Jesus begins by framing the point: "The kingdom is here with you"... But as you stubbornly miss it; you will look and look in vain... for a long time. However, when the Son of Man does come again, you will all know it; it will be impossible for you to miss Him. So, the kingdom is here. And Messiah Jesus will come again... but not yet in the way you are thinking.

Then Jesus gives the context to this teaching: He references two prior divine judgment/destruction/salvation events. In Noah's time, God destroyed the sinful world population, its buildings, its masterpieces, its arts and erased all traces of that population and its culture... yet He saved His faithful people. The second event is when God destroyed the population of Sodom and Gomorrah, its culture, its buildings and pulverized any trace of it. Yet He saved Lot's family. The context of Luke is judgment, and destruction for the purpose of selective salvation.

Having framed the subject, Jesus tells them that it is exactly how it will be when the Son of Man comes again. And indeed, through Daniel 2, Ezekiel and the other prophets, the Hebrews can expect the same divine cataclysmic, visible effects when Jesus comes to carry out the destruction of the last human supra-national empire (not a trace of it and of the other supra-national empires will be found—just as in the flood and Sodom). As part of the process, Jesus will judge the Hebrews. The judgment will be about His covenant (Jesus as Messiah). And then, powerfully, majestically, in sight of all humanity, Jesus will save the

Hebrews who embraced Him as Messiah and He will move them to the land of Israel that He has allotted them: We see judgment/destruction/salvation.

Jesus' actions will be on a divine scale, with divine means and divine power. It will be inescapable. Jesus is clear: Don't try to flee or to protect yourself—that would be useless. Jesus will find you wherever you are; from the intimacy of your bed to the camaraderie of your activities. There will be no escape.

"... *But whoever gives his life will save it*": Every Hebrew who will give up his life to Jesus at that time will be saved throughout the process. (They will have seen Him; but will not yet know Him intimately and deeply. The Messianic Jews will take care of that once in Israel, bringing out the good of the old and the good of the new... to their brethren.)

As Daniel 2 foretells, the divine strike will be universal; and it will be 100% accurate—even into the intimacy of your bed or the close camaraderie of your work—yet, there will be no collateral damage! (One will be taken, one will be left alive...) And, divine judgment will be undeterred: every Hebrew who turns down the proffered covenant will be destroyed (*taken*).

Hearing this, the people asked Jesus: *Where will this happen?* (Not when)... Probably meaning: Will it happen even in Jerusalem? Or just somewhere else? Where? Jesus tells them that it will be universal. There will be no human boundaries to this divine action—everywhere vultures gather above: A universal phenomenon.

So, yes of course, it will be useless to try to flee or to try to protect yourselves. The action will be universally evident yet intensely personal.

As we have seen so far in this essay, two of the steps of "God's march of glory" are deeply intertwined: the Rock breaking the One-World-Government/New-World-Order empire and the culling process of the Hebrews for exodus 2.0. The two may be facets of the same whole. The Old Testament scriptures carry through in time unerringly and Jesus, here, verifies these prophecies.

>Please note: Luke 17 is not about the rapture because at the rapture Jesus does not destroy people or things. At the rapture He joyfully harvests His own. The rapture is a happy time; not a retribution. Luke 17 is Hebrew centric; it is not for the Gentiles. Also, Luke 17 is not when Jesus comes back to reign for a thousand years because at that time, He only becomes visible after the great divine plagues of the tribulations have done their killing and destruction. At that time, He will come down majestically, in the joyful company of His saints, to reign. (Refer to *Revelation the Fair God*.) Finally, Luke 17 is not the battle of Armagedon and the mopping up action that follows this final battle because then, there will be no Gentile spared (there will not be "One taken and one left"...). And at that time, Jesus does not stay to fill the earth because He makes the earth disappear.

In Luke 20:13 – 19, Jesus also brings into focus what Daniel 2 had predicted. And in our time, with the long lens of elapsed history, we can see that Luke 20 ties up the following loose ends: "In what way are the Pharisaic Jews and their present day followers guilty?" And "Is the Jewish component of the Satanic One-World-Government/New-World-Order a central target for the rock-not-cut-by human hands, making the culling process of exodus 2.0 and the destruction of the fourth empire one and the same?"

The parable of the vineyard and the vineyard owner lays it all out clearly. In Jesus' time, the Pharisees—with the connivance of the teachers of the Law—had already highjacked the Jewish faith and they were ready to effect their evil workaround the Divine Messiah: God's beloved son. And what they thought (*Let's kill him so the inheritance will be ours*; verse 14) is what they did: they threw Jesus out of Jerusalem and killed Him. *Kill him so the inheritance will be ours* is the fitting short version of the One-World-Government/New-World-order's motto and modus operandi. Destroy Jesus and we will rule the world and the universe.

So, what did the Lord of the vineyard do? He did just as the parable said: All the Jewish people who rejected Jesus were thrown out of Jerusalem and out of the blessed land (circa AD 70 – 130)... And the good news was offered to the Gentiles. (It was never closed to the Jews: any descendant of Jacob could become of follower of Jesus at any time—and many have done so.)

Then, pointedly, Jesus ties in the process to Daniel 2. *The stone that the builders rejected, this has become the chief cornerstone. Whoever will fall against this stone will break his neck, and if that stone falls on [strike] someone, it will crush that person* (translated from B. d. S.) The Rock will indeed break the people of the last empire. Both the Jews (Hebrews) who reject Jesus and the Gentiles who have signed onto their programs.

Another telling detail is in the last part of verse 19: The Pharisees and the teachers of the Law understood very well that they were the target of this parable. ...Yet, tragically, they still went ahead with their evil plan to derail God's long appointed plan—what insane hubris!

The One-World-Government/New-World-Order of our era is just the latest—and it will be the ultimate—iteration of this Satanic/Luciferian human hubris. The movers and shakers of this movement—Jewish and Gentiles—who adhere to it, will be crushed by the very Stone they discarded and had committed to by-passing. The New-World-Order is not new; its pharisaic roots are over two thousand years old.

In scriptures, God promised the Hebrews a millennium of blessed hegemony under the rule of God's Messiah. However the Jews of Jesus' time rejected Messiah when He clearly revealed Himself and accomplished His prophesied messianic destiny. So, those who have rejected Messiah—and those who will reject Him—will not participate in the wonderful millennium of blessings. A couple of centuries ago, knowing, or sensing that this avenue would be closed to them, these rebellious people endeavored to make their dominant empire happen on their own terms. Adam and later Nimrod had tried the same approach. So, have the Globalists through their One-World-Government/New-World-Order.

Note: The promised 1,000 year reign will happen just as God meant it to happen. But all the real Hebrews who reject Jesus (that is: the new covenant as presented to them) will have been destroyed by Jesus as part of the process leading to exodus 2.0. They will not participate in anything on this earth again. These doomed souls will only leave Hades' limbo to receive their eternal bodies after the thousand year reign and to face their sentencing to Hell at the Great White Throne—along with every rebellious Gentile.

Note: This section is not the expression of an antisemitic spirit on my part. It simply reflects the facts that I could gather from what I read. I remain jubilant about the wonderful blessings God has planned for his righteous ancient people. But, God always deals with His people; they do not get a free pass on rebellion. I encourage you to read and search so you can come to your own conclusions. I am wholeheartedly for the righteous exodus 2.0 and I root for the Hebrews. But I left the wagon of delusion that demands that I'd make the current State of Israel (that began in 1948) the fulfillment of the glorious, divine prophetic return of the Hebrews to the land of Israel.

Weaving these threads into a practical whole

Having established that:

- There seems to be a Hebraic component at the root (and at the top) of the evil Globalist cabal, and

- The Globalists' Deep State is antipodal to Jesus and committed to prevent Jesus' plan, and

- The Hebrews do live in every country of the world today, and

- There are Hebrews living in the State of Israel as well, and

- The Globalists' One-World-Government/New-World-Order is the controlling human power in all the countries where most of the Hebrews live, and

- The Globalists' One-World-Government/New-World-Order is also the controlling power in the State of Israel where the rest of the Hebrews live

We find that we now have a situational similarity with God's setting in Moses' time when the power structure opposing God applied to every living Hebrew (they all lived in Egypt then). Today, for only the second time in history, we also have an overbearingly powerful structure that applies to every living Hebrew, wherever they may live—including in the State of Israel. The difference is that today's overbearing power also claims a Hebraic ascendency.

Ezekiel tells us that God will do all these things in our later years so that people everywhere will see Him; this is the whole point of the process. Moses did the same: He kept revealing YHWH, the God of heaven and earth. His people needed to know YHWH and so did Pharaoh (Pharaoh said: *Who is this YHWH? Why should I obey Him?*). With every plague, God, through Moses, showed who He is. Moses was the pointer, but God was the doer.

Interestingly, Moses did not ask Pharaoh to let God's people leave for good; but to have the opportunity to go worship the God of heaven and earth—effectively pointing to God and only to God. The entire process of the plagues was to reveal the true God; it was all about God. The God that the Hebrews had forgotten and the God the rest of humanity needed to know. So, in our time, when the rock breaks the legs of iron and clay, it will also be to reveal the God of heaven and earth and His son Messiah... To the Hebrews—real or pretenders—who dismissed Him and also to the rest of humanity.

King Nebuchadnezzar's dream and the prophetic pronouncements of Daniel felt incongruous within the biblical text, because unlike the rest of the old testament prophecies, it did not seem to refer or apply to God's ancient people at all. Yet, in our era, for the first time in history, we have the supra-national controlling entity that corresponds precisely to Daniel's description, and, lo and behold, it is "Jewish" at its core. In this light, Daniel 2 ceases to be an oddity and joins the rank of all the other old testament prophecies: It is Hebrew centric.

In Moses' time, the Pharaonic Egyptian power structure brought the wrath of God on itself and its people, this time the relevant power will be smashed by the same God.

> Note: An interesting parallel: At exodus 1.0 from Egypt, God destroyed the opposing kingdom. Was this divine action a precursor, a prototype, for the "Rock" that will

break the fourth empire? Consider the following: In Egypt, the Hebrews were outside their God-promised land and in servitude to Egypt. When Daniel 2 prophecy was given, the Jews were outside their God-given land and were subjects of Nebuchadnezzar's Babylonian Empire. And today, the Jews in large part (and the ten tribes in toto) are outside the land of promise. They are, just as we are, captive in the fourth empire. (It is the same for the Messianic Jews within the State of Israel; they are captive of the Globalists' New-World-Order that rule that state.)

So, what do we have?

- We know that the fourth empire will be divinely destroyed—presently.

- We know that the rebellious Hebrews will be destroyed by God before Jesus takes the entire faithful remnant into the land of Israel.

- We also know that there is an intrinsic Hebraic core to this fourth empire.

So, can we assume or conclude that the destruction of the fourth empire of Daniel 2 and the destruction of the Hebrew rebels for exodus 2.0 of Ezekiel 20:33 – 38 are part of the same process—or even the process itself? You decide; but I think that it is a possibility.

The above thoughts offer an interesting possibility: will God/Jesus use a series of well-defined, well-aimed plagues to destroy the power of the Globalists this time too? I don't know, but it is a possibility. Habakkuk 3:5, 6a, and 13 give us an idea: *The sickness went before him, and the destroyer followed behind him. He stood and judged the earth. He looked at the people of all the nations, and they shook with fear... You came to save your people and to lead your chosen king to victory. You killed the leader in every evil family, from the least important person to the most important in the land...*

So, students of the Bible, followers of Jesus, we should be awake and aware of what is happening to be able to identify each of these plagues for what it is. Our preparedness will enable us to encourage our brethren to offer glorious praises to the Almighty God of heaven and earth. These plagues will be the demo-days (demolition days) of all ages, taking down the old, rotten structure, clearing the way for the glorious rebuild.

Our beloved America

What about the United States of America? Our country seems to fall further and further under the control of this immoral cabal as they destroy more and more tenets of our identity and values. Why are we, Americans, the target of the One-World-Government/New-World-Order's deconstruction frenzy? One of the reasons is that the Globalists have pretty much finished their overtaking task in other countries and can concentrate their fury on us. But there are more reasons for it:

The concentrated push of the One-World-Government empire against America began almost as soon as The United States became a country. By definition, "a nation under God" was the Satanic Cabal's enemy. By devious and evil ways, the evil elite have sought to subjugate the growing country and when parts of America proved resilient, they endeavored to corrupt the whole, to compromise it, ruin it and destroy it.

So, as a country, we are an oddity: on the one hand God has abundantly blessed our land and our people throughout the entire existence of the United States of America—because it pleased Him to do so for the nation under God. (Nation which never lost its core of true believers to this day.) And because of God's favor, the Satanic empire has systematically undermined the country and our people precisely because these people hate God and His followers. So while the good side has done astounding good things for the world (missions, generous assistance, open armed welcome...); the bad side has made us the enemy of the same things. As the good side sees Jesus as the Truth, and the Truth makes us free. The bad side has suborned every truth possible and reeled back every freedom we are endowed with.

The Globalists' cabal astutely identified the gap in our national armor and they poured their resources through it. This is what I mean: America's government is for the people and by the people therefore representatives are elected by the people. The term "Representative" has become a misnomer for the selfish climbers that have filled our institutions over time. Ambitious politicians hate fair elections because they fear elections. (They say they like fair elections when they know they are overwhelmingly popular or have securely rigged them; but those are the only instance they do.) Politicians of every hue hate to leave their self-appointed fate to the whim of the people out there. At any given election most of the politicians are up for re-election; that is: the continuance of their ambition is on the block. A citizen who thinks his representative/senator/governor/etc. wants fair elections is a naive person who has another think coming.

So, the politicians organized themselves into political parties, which are simply devices geared to control, influence, finance, and yes: rig, elections. That is it. Political parties have no other useful functions—none!

In monarchies, the Satanic cabal has one asset to leverage: the crown; but in a democracy/republic they have as many assets as there are political parties that they can leverage. Political parties are always looking for sources of plentiful, easy money; which is exactly whom the cabal looks to subvert. And by doing that, our venal or ambitious few have opened wide the door into the heart of America to the manipulators, the corrupters of the lawless One-World Cabal; who have put their nefarious skills to devastating use. These evil manipulators have invaded our congress, our agencies, our corporations and all levels of our administration and courts.

The Fourth Empire malevolently fomented our Civil War for which it financed both sides. The same Cabal got us involved in WWI, then

WW2, then in a multitude of wars, under our own banner or by proxies—while they financed every side of every conflict. Finances for which they collect systematically from us... placing a heavier and heavier burden on us, the people.

They engineered multiple financial collapses to ruin our masses and push new controls upon us. They highjacked our money in order to base their fiat money on the American dollar; in this way, they have associated us with the worldwide tyranny of corruption they have wrought. But they separated the dollars they printed and they placed an incredible amount of them out of reach of the American controls and laws as the Eurodollar (not to be confused with the Euro). The Eurodollar being the paper currency we are ruthlessly indebted to, but about which we cannot do anything because it is held and traded outside the US, outside our purview—and outside our system of laws, checks-and-balances.

They denigrated our enthusiastic and productive pioneers who ran the private, small businesses that built our country and replaced them with the modern CEOs—the professional social climbers. Corporate top-heavy overhead has replaced the spontaneous and diversified engines of progress that made America lively and competitive in every field.

They killed the small businesses because these are the bulwarks of national independence and self-reliance. The small businesses' existence is rooted in the very soil of their culture; they do not respond well to the top-down control the Globalists insist upon. These small, self-sufficient and usually effective businesses provided the people with endlessly adaptive solutions for their evolving needs.

Our overlords replaced the small businesses with cumbersome and wasteful behemoth corporations that they shield from open competition thus seriously limiting the number of sources and choices for the people at large. Our overlords can affect the availability of all supplies necessary for everyday life with one phone call to these beholden monopolistic behemoths. They can affect the quality and the goodness of what we ingest and what we wear by flexing their ascendence and control over the large, multinational corporations. We have seen this in real time when they used a "pandemic" to deal a death blow to hundred of thousands small businesses while enhancing and protecting—and richly rewarding—the wasteful, industrial giants. But, why are these giants so dear to our elite? Because they wield enormous amount of financing clout that they sprinkle back upon their obedient law-making politicians.

Large public corporations are absolutely enslaved to the fortunes of Wall Street. They live on the same chicaneries of money manipulations and speculations that this evil empire is built upon and set to function. They are just as vulnerable and subservient to the control of the Globalist bankers as the politicians are! The Globalists replaced our money with their fiat currency and they continually charge us for it!

They also tore at the moral fiber of American society in every way imaginable. Unfortunately, they found readily available kindling for their destructive flames. Our politicians greedily—and stupidly—bought into their schemes. These treacherously ambitious Americans connived to defraud their own brethren and co-citizens and so they did. Venal judges sold their integrity to insure their coveted seat on the various benches, a transaction they repay by shielding the guilty and penalizing the innocent according to their puppet masters' will. Academia was a very easy and willing prey to the lures of the cabal.

Treacherous politicians sent their own citizens to die or be maimed in irrelevant, pre-arranged, conflicts that have never solved anything. These venal, American traitors committed mass murder in the service of their international overlords. Over the last century the American press was bought and the people lost their traditional sources of relevant information. Our military academies have taught this elite's poison, so did our universities.

We passed laws that clearly had only one purpose: to weaken America... As well as to stick our finger in God's eye (abortion, divorce, LBGTQ, transgenderism...) We are duplicating what the hapless French did during their first revolution. We should have learned from history.

So, the Globalists' cabal has targeted America as the strategic linchpin of its ambitions, for, as long as America is not neutralized and its one-nation-under-God ideals not rejected, the whole plot remains precarious. The Globalists aim to destroy our country.

The core of the US has been the opposite of this fourth empire. Because it offered hope, a chance to progress, it naturally attracted millions who wanted a chance at their destiny. The US was the antithesis of the New-World-Order; it offered the right for people to own property as opposed to the people being owned. We can either own property; or we become the property... of someone else. The US offered the opportunity to be what God made us to be: His property; and no one else's. This is why the US was a magnet.

Because the United States always had immense resources and innate potential, plus was blessed with a huge workforce willing to toil, and has the ability to produce huge quantities of war material; the global elite worked relentlessly to neuter (all the time) and destroy (finally) America. The Globalists' One-World-Government focused on the insidious and relentless invasion of America at all levels and all functions—here we call it the Deep State. It seeped into all areas of our lives.

America was a main prize to attain. However, while other countries have completely fallen, the United States is still teetering on the edge:

enough of its people are holding onto their Christian core-identity and are preventing the cascading, fatal fall.

Our guilt As a nation

Unfortunately, the One-World-Government has damned America by making it its global bludgeon. A bludgeon it has wielded at will. In and throughout the history of the United States, these Globalists have used their patsies in our midst to wage wars in our name on all continents, to coerce famines, to export moral filth and to corrupt other societies.

The United States has killed more people directly (through abortions and our own wars) and by proxy (through sponsored foreign abortions, famines and exported conflicts) than any other nation on earth—ever. Ponder this. We self-righteously quote the 60 millions Mao starved in China, the 20 millions Stalin killed in the USSR; but these tyrants are lightweight when we consider our own record of wars, plus abortions, plus famines and plus systematic impositions of anti-health measures. As a nation, the United States of America truly reflect the foretold reality of the strength of iron as a destructive weapon. As the bludgeon of the fourth empire, we have indeed wrought destruction; and in doing so, we have earned the guilt thereof.

So, can we, as a country, hope to extricate ourselves from the doom that was pre-ordained in Daniel's time for our human supra-national masters? No, not anymore than we can scoop a glassful of clean water out of a polluted barrel. Our system is a microcosm of the Global Elite, we reflect its nature: crushing like iron and brittle like clay.

Instead of using our Christian faith as the cement of our American society—as the founders hoped we would—we have faltered and gotten loose. Now, we too are indeed divided. We were divided on the matters of slavery and state rights, we were divided during the Viet Nam war and others conflicts. We are divided about abortion (yes, the majority of us—God-fearing Americans—oppose it). By governmental manipulations, we are divided on racial lines and on gender lines. We are deeply divided on just about every issue. And our elite strives to deepen and exploit every possible crack in our societal character. A prescient Daniel reported above: *People will mix with one another, but they will not adhere to one another...* A description that now fits us, Americans, as it fits the Globalists' empire.

However, contrarily to many smaller countries that had lesser means to resist the evil cabal, the United States of America has a significant population of citizens who—when push comes to shove—will choose to oppose this construct by following their beloved Lord Jesus. This is whom the cabal fear. Indeed, we have a large number of true followers of Jesus. (I am not talking about denomination affiliation or traditional church attenders or the Christians-in-name-only who readily accommodate evil; I am talking about the deeply committed and serious souls who identify with Jesus, embrace His will and obey His commands... And walk where their Lord walks.) And this is where the fight is: they want to crush us because as long as there exist live embers, the flames of God's kingdom can leap forth again ... We can be assured: God knows it; He sees us. The very God who has showered our people and land with His sustained blessings knows every one who is His. When Jesus hits the evil fourth empire, the true Christian core will not be destroyed.

As a founding principle, and for a long while, America kept the spiritual beliefs of its people off-limits to the state's control; but gradually, the state eroded all this, turned the premise on its head and appropriated it. Today, our system is not distinguishable from the Globalists dictates, and from scriptures we see that we are now identified with Nebuchadnezzar's spiritual over-reach that is common to these four empires. As a system, we are now guilty of this as well.

The Globalists' evil cabal has been after us, American Christians, for more than two centuries; and yet, a core of us is still here... vibrant and praying. We, believers are not the problem for God; we are the ones He is very pleased with—the ones He adopted and watches for. In what's coming, He will carry His followers through. To wit: In Moses' time, the Hebrews (God's people) made it unscathed through the divine destruction of the Egyptian system. At that time, God's people marched on, led and protected by God, onto a new system. Many had trouble letting go of the Egyptian system they were familiar with; but the new system was God's chosen reality for them. So it will be for us.

Very soon, as in "before He effects exodus 2.0" Jesus will act on this matter. When Jesus strikes, the Globalists' One-World-Government/One-World-Order will disappear without leaving as much as a footprint. And with it, so will the American system it has compromised. The bad, corrupt actors in our midst that the Globalists have purchased and commanded will lose everything—and I mean everything.

It has to be that way

The American system as we have come to experience it—not the system our forefathers had envisioned—will be gone. None of the optimistic slogans that populate social media or the many influencers' blue-sky promises will protect against or deflect the coming destruction of the America we have become. The process of transiting America from today's cesspool into tomorrow's better nation will not be done by well-meaning, good people who are finally able to turn the corner around wickedness and proceed unhampered to a restoration of what used to be. What used to be will be gone, just as Daniel said it would be, long ago. God said He would do this. So He will; not us. And Jesus' regime will be the only worldwide regime from then on (*the stone that struck the image became a great mountain and filled the whole earth*).

However, in the short time until God destroys the Cabal's fourth empire, we, who identify with Him, must personally stand on our spiritual convictions and principles and reject, in every way, the evil empire's moral encroachment, day by day and item by item. We can neither accommodate, nor can we submit. We cannot misapply Proverb 20:3: *Avoiding a fight is a mark of honor; only fools insist on quarreling* (NLT); to justify our cowardliness. This verse applies to everyday conflicts—usually motivated by selfish gains; not the fight against pure evil. Regarding the fourth empire, we do not need to fight (God will do that) but we must not accommodate. Daniel did not fight, but he did not accommodate in any way: He prayed as always. Meshach, Shadrach and Abednego did not fight; but they did not accommodate in any way.

And we cannot become silent. What the evil empire pushes down on us goes against what God demands of us. So, if we are His, we must refuse, we must say no in the public square and in our own homes. Meshach, Shadrach and Abednego were not silent: ... *But even if God does not save us, we want you O king, to know this: We will not serve your gods or worship the gold statue you have set* up (Daniel 3:18).

The same thing happened with Peter and John when the very same cabal of Satanic Talmudic Jewish leaders who aims to rule today forbade them to say anything or teach anything in the name of Jesus. Peter was not silent, Peter did not compromise: *Should we obey you or God? We cannot be quiet...* (Acts 4:18 – 20). That was up-front and in-your-face courage. They laid it clearly for all to hear... And in doing so, they cleared the way for God to act. In every of these historical cases, had the righteous compromised, there would not have been any reason for God to intervene; because it would have been simply a matter of people accommodating idolatry, albeit with some coercion thrown in. Nothing has changed since then: Matthew 10:32 and Luke 12:8, *Everyone who acknowledge me publicly here on earth, I will also acknowledge before my Father in heaven. But everyone who denies me here on earth* [to win favor with the powers of men] *I will also deny before my father in heaven* (Matthew 10:32 – 33 NLT, insert mine). Jesus orders us to take the same uncompromising stance. There is nothing ambiguous about any of this.

An enigma resolved

Ezekiel chapters 38 and 39 have created an enigma for modern American Christians: There is no mention of America at all in and around the war of Gog and Magog against America's ally Israel; why?

Understanding the effects of Daniel 2 above gives us the answer: the America we have come to know will be irrelevant after the destruction of the Deep State/One-World-Government. Since 1948, the American Christians were roped in by the Satanic cabal to support and to identify with the State of Israel—the state this very cabal created. But, with the Rock's action, the American Christians will have experienced a full dose of scriptural reality, their eschatology will have been recalibrated, plus the humanistic State of Israel will not exist as such. So we as a country will have no import on God's majestic events. It is really as simple as that.

And finally, the Deep State warmongers among us will have been destroyed. They will not be the usual trumpeting for war. They will not be here to whip up the emotions of the country for war. That era will be gone, gone for good (literally: for the good).

After the Rock's action and exodus 2.0, our free and cleansed country will be in overload of emotions, energies and focus as we will be a spectator of God's continued action overseas. And our Christians will be in a state of praise. The only countries that Ezekiel mentions in the

Gog and Magog chapters are Muslim countries; by their religion, they are relevant to the action; but we won't be.

This must be a personal matter, not a group thing

Ours must be a personal, individual commitment and walk. The key words are "personal" and "individual".

Efforts to unite under associations, action groups or branded movements are counter productive: it only gives a bigger, and a centralized target to the enemy. We cannot fight the human fight that the enemies are well prepared for and equipped to do. It would be giving up the high ground and striking out of the umbrella of defense that God provides for His followers—for each and every one of us. It would be entering the boggy trap of the entrenched enemy's choosing. Our strength and safety is in Jesus alone; trying to build a human bulwark, a collective, protective armor, brings us down into the realm of the enemy's expertise and its entrapping quagmire... the field where he excels and we lose.

Every association, and action group is made up of good people, mediocre people and some loonies. These imperfect groupings offer excellent opportunity for the disingenuous empire to pick one bad apple and, through their captive press, paint the whole group as a multiple of the same—tarnishing and even ostracizing thousands or tens of thousands legitimate, upstanding folks. Associations, action groups afford the Deep State unlimited leverage over the masses. It takes just a few targets to label a large group as "terrorist organization".

We, God's people, are far more effective individually, personally. The Deep State cannot publish millions of lists of lone individuals as terrorist organizations. The three Hebrew exiles above did not try to rally the righteous masses, to get a large group of sympathizers organized to offer a "larger resistance" to Nebuchadnezzar's edict; and they were right. God does not need a human multiplier to do His thing: He usually accomplish His work through the lone, committed follower. The catch is that being God's man demands personal courage. Courage is not the absence of fear; courage is having the mettle to act rightly in the overbearing presence of fear. And courage has been denigrated in our society, the courageous person is labelled as insensitive, selfish, judgmental—a social misfit... And the cowardly sycophant is idolized and promoted.

Plus, there is another dimension that has become evident recently, especially since the advent of the internet: Organizing movements or groups only feeds the egos and agendas of a new, and different class of opportunists. People who do not have the upper hand today, who may be marginally relevant; can gain fortune, fame and influence through a group. Just a new twist to the same old problem. The internet is redolent of these opportunists—influencers, they are called.

When we ignore God's way; we can expect man's way. And that's never good for God's people.

This above principle applies in the profane just as it applies in the spiritual domain. Take the trade unions. Workers were told that if they unionized, they would be represented and have power—numbers make power, right? This too was a trap. Union bosses, as history proves over and again, are easily corrupted and cheap to suborn. This is what happened, the nefarious Global elite bought the bosses and the masses were sold a false security and received fleeting, non-essential benefits. For example: the bosses angrily whipped their members to demand higher wages, so union factory workers received higher wages; good, right? But what was the overall goal of the Globalists? It was to impoverish the industrialized world and to create millions of dependent and despondent former workers at the mercy of the State's for their care. So, what was the real upshot of the unionized trick? Higher wages provided the impetus for the Globalists to carry out the transfer of useful manufacturing out to other parts of the world; leaving an idle and empty rust belt in our country. The union members got crumbs and celebrated, the elite laughed: they had won big! Workers did not need to unite; they needed to personally act on their beliefs and accept the responsibility of their lives, their skills and their talents. When we elect to play in the devil's sandbox; we can only expect sand in our teeth and in our eyes.

Earlier in the text you read that the human being is created to be horizontally responsible and vertically led; there is a third component to this divine principle of creation: Protection. God is our only protection, our fortress. He is not our "last refuge"; the one we retreat to when we have exhausted all other human means of defense. He created the principle that He is our personal defender, our personal rampart, our personal savior in all situations—from the smallest threat to the most dire impending disaster. We should not seek our safety, our safe-conduct on the horizontal level; that is through groups, governments, institutions... If we do, we forsake true safety and abandon our fate to illusion. We walk into the ancient trap. The bible is replete of examples of this.

Associating and organizing gives the individual a false sense of security in numbers. The reality of the Good News is that each individual believer has to build his own strength by relentlessly practicing the Way of Jesus. Jesus didn't say to Peter: Assemble a very powerful group and follow Me. He said: As for you, follow Me.

The tools of the enemy (mass media, government administration, political PACs, Hollywood, surveillance and repressive agencies) are tools created and trained to influence and combat massed oppositions, to put out large forest fires and to reap the news value of it all. However these same means are pitifully unadapted to putting out millions of independent, persistent, disparate and self-generating, self-sustaining fires. The omnipotent, omnipresent and omniscient God can lead, protect and place every one of these individual fiery brands. We cannot be a part of His fight by using the enemy's weapons and tactics.

We have Noah's example to help us: Noah lived at the cusp of God's terrible judgement on humanity and creation; and what do we know about him? *And God punished the world long ago when He brought a flood to the world that was full of people who were against Him. But God saved Noah, who preached about being right with God...* (2 Peter 2:5 NCV). Noah did not "go along to get along". Noah did not fly under the radar, pretending to be part of the rest. Not only did he not join in the Satanic spirit of the time; he preached against it. He was not silent!

In staking his stand for what was right; Noah did not try in vain to create a coalition to help him. Can we expect for one moment that Noah was never threatened? That his life was not in danger? Impossible; he was bringing out the truth and truth has only two effects on people: either repentance (as David did when confronted by Nathan) or unbridled anger and savage murderous rage against the messenger (this is the root of the killing of Christians by Muslims in Africa or by Hindus in Asia). Obviously, popular repentance was never the case in Noah's time; so, by inference, we can expect that he faced savage, murderous rage. But the powers of that time did not prevail against this one man. Think of the odds: One man versus the entire world. Similarly, Moses was God's one man against Pharaoh and his multi-faceted might (Moses' own people did not even rally behind him). Yet, Moses prevailed.

> <u>Note</u>: From influencers, I hear and read: "we, the good guys" outnumber "they, the bad guys"; so we are going to win. If associating, ganging up, building a majority was the key to overcome; wouldn't it logically ensue that "we", by virtue of numbers, would be in power? The reality is: "we" are not in

power. And with my limited scope of history, it seems that this is usually the case everywhere, any time: the minority always rules. And when its grip is threatened, it cheats to regain it, it lies to do so, it goes to war to do so, it represses to do so. Based on history, our chances of reversing the present situation by the association of "we, the people" are not realistic. The minority has had decades (at least) to imagine, to perfect and to hone the tools that control us. Just as Biden said before the last election: they were ready to cheat like never before, they had perfected multi-prong programs—they were not sweating it. He was correct. "We, the majority" lost to "they, the minority"; and "they" still rule (2023).

We are the mirrors, so let us Reflect, reflect, reflect

Our situation today is getting dire, the murderous rage is building; but the mettle of the actors has not changed. They are still the useful idiots of the same old enemy. What has changed is that the world at large now knows about the universal Truth of Jesus and consciously rejects it and squashes it. The hundreds of millions of followers of Jesus, expounders of the Truth are the mirrors that reflectively expose the rot within the rebellious; the rot these people assiduously bury.

Everywhere they turn, there are mirrors, mirrors, always mirrors... It is maddening for them. So, they break the mirrors, they legislate the existence of the mirrors away, they outlaw the mirrors and they encourage their minions to destroy the mirrors everywhere they find them. It used to be that gross sin was "in the closet"; now gross sin parades on Main Street and it demands that the revealing mirrors be permanently locked in closets.

But as history records: Our enemy will lose—he always does. And our LORD is able to protect us as He protected Noah—day in and day out for one hundred years while Noah built the ark. God protected Moses; His one-man-with-a-stick. But if we cowardly identify or cooperate with the doomed losers, if we agree to put our light under the bed; we will share their fate. We have been warned; we have no excuses—none. Each one of us must reflect the light.

Our bible is replete with dependable prototypes. As listed above, we have Noah, Moses, David, the three exiles, and Daniel... Their personal faithfulness brought them under the special protection of God Almighty. Not only them, but the rest of their people were collectively protected and blessed because of these individuals' uncompromising stands. Looking again, specifically to the three exiles: What would have happened to them and their people had they cowered and justified their compromising as: "It is the law; we cannot go against the law, it would not be right. We don't make the laws; so what choices do we have? We have to be good citizens. God puts these rulers over us; we must respect their demands." What would have been their outcome if they had acted cowardly like so many of us American Church-ians have done on so many issues?

At another juncture, within the same empire, it is Daniel who personally, individually disobeyed the law of the king and by doing so brought down the power of heavens for his protection and eventually the protection of his people. He faced the human punishment of a savage death by lions; but as recorded: no punishment can get by God's protective hand.

So, in the times of our supra-national empire, we have no spiritual basis to give in because what the One-World-Order demand is against the will of God. Plus, in America, we have no tactical or legal reason to submit and join these elites because they are the ones who constantly break our established laws! We have no spiritual basis to be silent; and we have no legal basis either. So, let's not be cowards; cowardice in today's situation is the first attribute that will damn people: *But cowards who turn away from Me...their doom is in the lake that burn with fire and sulfur* (Revelation 21:8 NLT)

Our witness matters: While we might not change others' mind; they will keep hearing the truth. They will have to willfully shut their eyes to the light we reflect; thus condemning themselves. And God will count us as His.

We cannot humanly fight and defeat the fourth empire anymore than Daniel, Shadrach, Meshach and Abednego could fight and vanquish the first. We are not asked to do so. Especially since God unveiled his plan for the destruction of this very empire more than two millennia ago.

Looking ahead, our current struggle is our believers' training ground. When this evil empire is gone, we will need a base of clear-thinking, solid, courageous and committed believers who truly know Jesus and who will contribute to build our nation under Jesus' guidance. We will need people who will have validated their moral compass in adversity. Our current difficult time is our "boot camp"; it sifts our faith, cleans our game and builds our stand. It trains us to speak the truth even if truth is not received. It turns our heads toward Him whence our directions will come.

We must never lose track of the fact that the actual destruction of the Globalists' empire and its Deep State cohort will not be our work. Only God can root it out. The evil empire is so enmeshed, so intimately woven into the very fibers of our country that its death will drag our system down with it. We must disassociate from it now; we are not of it...we are of what is coming after it. We are of the stone that will fill the earth.

Why is it so hard Now?

The unpleasant choking of our lives that the evil empire ratchets down relentlessly should not surprise the believer. As demoralizing as it may get, we must recognize it for what it is by understanding that the same unpleasantness was present during the first exodus as the Enemy vainly thought to derail God's plan. When Moses began his task, God allowed Pharaoh to ramp up the miseries of the Israelites' slavery. God allowed depressing, demoralizing duress on the Hebrews—His people—to get their attention. Indeed, before applying the devastating plagues onto the Egyptians, God allowed some time and did some miracles to get His people to focus on Him.

However, the Hebrews had drunk the Kool-aid of slave-hood. They did not want to upset their human masters. They only hoped that by compromising endlessly, by slavishly submitting, they could maintain the status quo—poor as it was. They believed their safety and defense were exclusively at the human level... Then, this crazy guy, Moses, appeared and upset the situation.

Moses spoke to the Hebrews about their rightful God and about their imminent liberation and transfer to their promise land. And Moses stood up to Pharaoh and his administration. Pharaoh reacted by making life hopeless and pitiful for the Hebraic population. This is what the fourth empire and its Deep State are doing to us in our days. Our rights are abrogated daily, our margins of freedom are being cut, then cut again, our property and wealth are devaluated... The bar of our fealty is reset higher and higher... Like in Egypt: it is becoming depressing for the good people.

The elite and their administration are making it tougher for the good people, the followers of Jesus—like Pharaoh, they see us as slaves. How dare we oppose their will? They aim to put us back in our box. For a short few years, there was a fresh wind, an awakening, in our nation; so now, they make us pay for it. But the wind of righteous freedom blew through the tinder that was ready, and a righteous fire is spreading.

And just as in Moses' time: Whom do the gutless "sheeples" of our time resent? Just like the Hebrews of old, our co-citizens do not resent the tyrants who impose these unfair, severe orders; instead they turn against the righteous and courageous opposers who seem to be the reason and the root of their discomfort! In a typical cowardly fashion, they universally turned against the hope-givers to pacify the oppressors! Can you see it?

Here is an example, today (2023), a strong American individual stood (2016) and went toe-to-toe against the Globalist cabal and the Globalist cabal turned on him and are tightening the screws on the "rabble"; in the same swoop, making life more and more miserable for all the "sheeples". And predictably, most of the sheeple have turned against the courageous man: they are afraid that his "rocking the boat" would swamp their not-so-comfy nests.

Today, our cowardly, and often effeminate clergy, our cowardly congregations and our compromised believers have folded shamefully. They have prostrated themselves in servile dehumanizing fashion at the foot of these Satanists... They have befouled the immutable commands and tenets of their faith in order to pacify the evil masters. They have abandoned the clear moral principles commanded in the word of God and prostituted themselves at the altar of depravity.

They have withdrawn from the commands to stand firm, they have abdicated the faith that would single them out and instead have cloistered themselves into preaching a non-offensive gospel. They pontificate on the non issues. By this they have disqualified themselves as shepherds... And they have turned against the messengers and against the people who responded and rose to the hope. The cowardly accommodators always aim too squeak by unnoticed and unmolested;

in this they are deluded. This "church" will have to be cleansed of that cancerous layer.

It seems to me that God is allowing the progressive hardening of the state against Christians. It appears to me that the forcible constraints that the Deep State continually imposes upon us have the same purpose it had in Egypt: to wake us up and to build God's audience. Without this, we would continue to be distracted and miss God's glorious deeds. We would not give Him the glory when He conducts the destroying actions that will accompany exodus 2.0. This tightening of the Globalists' noose around our necks is meant to wake us up, to turn our eyes to God and to stand up, seeking wisdom in scriptures. It is meant to switch our hope on Him and abandon all illusions of human solutions or provisions.

Those who refuse Him also need to be ready to see what is happening so that, willing or not, they will know that the credit goes to Jesus—and not to fate. What we, believers, say and do will plant this awareness in them.

It will be worth it

This struggle is worth it. The text is clear: This destructive empire will be absolutely pulverized and there will not be a fifth supra-national empire after the Globalists'. This not a temporary hiatus, it will not be followed by the same dismal slide into the depressing pit we live under now. Human supra-national empires (like the gold, silver, bronze or iron) are finished. Life available to us after this divine action will be on a basis not seen since the garden of Eden. It will not begin a cycle of the same old routine as we had after WWI, or WWII. This is really worth it.

However, this will not be a reprieve from all adversity because sin will still be present but the change will nevertheless be transformational.

The Globalists' One-World-Order is the last one; there will never be another—American or otherwise. No wonder the elites push so hard! Desperately, they think they can race God and escape His reach.

But escaping God's reach is not going to happen. When Jesus has dealt with them, He will rule... And countries will again be countries, independent and self-determined—all functioning with Jesus as the only supra-national arbiter... for the last few years remaining of our era. (Note: As arbiter, not as absolute Lord as He will during the millennium.) After breaking the empire, executing exodus 2.0 and Gog and Magog, Jesus will be the focus of discussions. He will be the matter at stake.

The upside for us in America is that we can finally expect a type of government our ancestors could only dream of. And, the Globalists' New-World-Order having been destroyed, America—as all countries—will be independent and sovereign...under Jesus' assurance. And this is the era when our Christ-following, good people, will come into play for the "great harvest" (covered in the last part of this dissertation, or read *The Great Harvest of the Post-Allah World*).

The good news is: America will end up with an existential situation and a functional construct far better than what our human clean-up and restoration efforts could have cobbled together. I cannot predict what it will look like; but the faithful will be very glad and the wicked who survive will take notice. We, believers, will rejoice in our beautiful country... independent and sovereign, and united under God if we wish—*The land of the free and the home of the brave*. One thing that will be destroyed forever is our aggressive imperialism, our forcing our will over other countries—it was a sort of supra-national empire. It was what the fourth empire wielded America for. And that never truly represented the root population of our great country.

We are all aware of the slogan: Make America Great Again. An astute commentator recently proposed: Make America Godly Again. Whoever he/she is has transcended our current discourse and extracted the keystone of our future. When the gangrene of the Deep State (One-World-Government/New-World-Order) is scoured out, the slogan may simply be: Make America Great. Indeed, it will be an opportunity to develop what we never had a chance to get to. The few short years before the rapture and the great tribulations could be glorious indeed.

It will be better than ever before because we will have entered the times of God's joyful celebrations. He always shares His rejoicing (see the parable of the king's wedding banquet for his son). Ezekiel 38 and 39 tells us that God will rejoice in Israel with His regathered ancient people; and we can expect that He will rejoice in all the other theaters with His Gentile followers who will be very busy teaching others about the God they will all have seen in action. Ezekiel tells us that God will joyfully give bumper crops to the people in Israel, I think that we can expect similar largesses to extend to our side as well.

Finally, Ezekiel and other prophets have told us that the upcoming exodus of the Hebrews will be modeled after the exodus of Moses' time. Way back in Egypt, an overwhelmingly powerful, idolatrous regime was flattened by the All-powerful God of the defenseless Hebrews prior to the exit of His people from Egypt. The powerful, entrenched, all-invasive and pervasive power of the Globalists today will be slammed by the same God, <u>before</u> Jesus moves His ancient people out again.

We should take heart from the biblical prototype: in Egypt of antiquity, Satan had a very powerful human army—Pharaoh's army. For its time and place, it was an overwhelming force: thousands of chariots, officers, foot soldiers, it had all the swords, spears and bows in the land. God had a human army too: one old man with a stick. God managed the situation in a unique way: while God was destroying Egypt, Pharaoh was unable to use this powerful army. Indeed: how do you use an army against flies, boils, hail, disease or darkness?

And finally when Egypt was in smoldering ruins and its population in mourning, God, triumphantly, led His people out. At that juncture, Pharaoh thought that he could finally wield his army to overpower his retreating slaves...but for God's old man with his stick by the sea... Pharaoh lost everything he had left. While God crushes the evil empire of the Globalists, their worldly and military powers will be irrelevant as well. And theirs, like Pharaoh's, will be vanquished and destroyed—completely.

We live in the time of the great paradigm shift when the *stone, not cut by hands* smashes the kingdom of iron and clay and reaches through history to erase all traces of the *bronze, silver and gold* types of kingdom—they will be *crushed together*—there will not even be a trace of their having existed and functioned: *Not a trace of them could be found.*

We will begin a new era: *the God of heaven will set up a kingdom that will never be destroyed, nor will this kingdom be left to another people. It will crush and bring to an end all of these kingdoms. But it will endure forever. For just as you saw a stone cut out of a mountain, yet not by hands, crush the iron, bronze, clay, silver and gold, the great God has made known to the king what will happen in the future.*

This blessed series of events listed above will not yet be the 1,000 year earthly reign of Jesus, therefore, until then, evil will still be practiced at large (Satan will not be bound yet and his demons will still be present and active). Many people will still reject God in Jesus to pursue and serve the enemy of mankind. Many will be lured by the deceiver. However, what will be gone is the official sponsorship, the vertical imposition and enforced compliance of evil by legislation or executive orders—measures currently backed by the powers of our insidious, overbearing state and its institutions in the service of the overarching, supra-national government. That capability will never be recreated.

So, the pickle we are in will metamorphose into a blessed span of time when today's tyrants do not rule. And this blessed time takes effect in our time, some years before the rapture of Jesus' followers.

My fellow believers, there are indeed overwhelming biblical reasons and precedents to be optimistic in the near term. We need not be ignorant about this; God took the time and care to address the subject specifically and precisely. Let those with wisdom and understanding strengthen the faint-hearted. Let us all look up, whence the actions will come. Finally, let us leave Church-ianity and embrace Christ-ianity.

Habakkuk (ERV)

We have concentrated on the fourth empire from the standpoint of its inception, nature and destruction. Other passages in the Bible broaden our horizon to include practical dimensions.

Context

As an introduction to the next part, let's look at Habakkuk's two complaints: They resonate deeply with us. We can relate to what Habakkuk expresses: *How long, O LORD, must I call for help... I cry to You: Violence!... Why do you make me look at injustice? Why do You tolerate Wrong?... The law is paralyzed and justice never prevails... Justice is perverted... Why do you tolerate the treacherous? Why are you silent while the wicked swallow those more righteous than themselves?*

There is a poignant urgency in Habakkuk's address; it is something the true followers of Jesus feel keenly today. And when we read the prayer that Habakkuk lifts to God in the third chapter; we realize that he understood that the actions were not only for his time; but more so for the "later times" (our time).

And finally God's answer to Habakkuk stirred me to write this piece: *Write down what I show you. Write is clearly on a sign so that the message will be easy to read [or: write the vision clearly on tablets so that the person who reads it can run and tell others]. This message is about a special time in the future. This message is about the end, and it will come true. Just be patient and wait for it. That time will come; it will not be late.*

So, Habakkuk's message is not about what happened around and about the Babylon of antiquity; it is for us the denizens of the "time of the end". Even if it had not said *this message is about the end*; we would still be able to understand that it is thus because the events surrounding the end of the Babylonian Empire of Habakkuk 2 do not match the record of past history on the original empire (so Habakkuk's message was not meant for that one). So Habakkuk and Daniel 2 converge.

Therefore, through most of its text, when Habakkuk refers to *the Babylonians*, or *their city*, he refers to the **type** of Babylonian supra-national empire that will be present in the last days. Thus, it is my opinion that the information and prophecy of Habakkuk actually applies to the Globalist One-World-Government—the fourth empire of Daniel 2: the empire that is ruling during the time of the end. The last supra-national human empire to exist.

THE PART PLAYED BY THE RIGHTEOUS

Part one of this presentation about the last kingdom (fourth empire in the lineage of Babylon) covers the divine destruction of the Globalists, their evil construct and their means of power. It identifies the Babylonian Empire of Daniel's time as the model and prototype for the malevolent empire of our time.

In Habakkuk, we receive more pertinent details about the end of the Globalist's supra-national empire. Habakkuk writes about the Babylonian Empire of his time. But that empire is relevant to us as the prototype for the other three empires of Daniel 2.

With Daniel 2, we saw that the destruction of this evil empire will be divinely carried out. God confirms through Habakkuk that the destruction will be divinely meted. But, Habakkuk also tells us that there will be a part to be played by Jesus' faithful who are the victims of this evil Globalist Empire. The righteous will be looting the defeated cabal. Here are some of the verses that make this evident:

The ERV Bible has a good way with words for Habakkuk 2:4, it says: *This message cannot help those who refuse to listen to it, but those who are good will live because they believe it.* Interesting information, isn't it? It adds light to Peter's *It is most important for you to understand what will happen in the last days.*

There is a cleaving, a rending applied to the world's population in our time because this is a time of judgment. (This is not a time of healing; it is a time for consequences and divine justice.) It is the time for the reset—the divine reset. We can feel it more and more, everyday. Every news cycle brings in new elements. So, I think the process has begun; as the Romans used to say: Alea jacta est! The dice have rolled.

It is interesting to note that from all quarters the Western Christians are being exhorted—and even legislated—to be nice, to be inclusive. The ungodly insist on telling us how we should live in a godly fashion. Shallow believer bow the knee to fit in. In my own limited observation, our own pastors are generally cowards. They do not exhibit the courage of the good shepherds in the Bible (as young David was). Taking a stand would put them out of their comfort zone and push them out of their carefully constructed community image of "niceness". Most of them, simply steer away from the subject. The few courageous ones are hounded and even prosecuted, here in America and also in Canada, they are rare beacons.

Yet, this is the time, on God's clock, when the population is been sorted into two groups. So, the time for indiscriminate inclusion is over (it was never a Christian principle anyway). However, the true righteous will be protected and will flourish. They believed, then they stood and they acted on their beliefs. The Globalist cabal means to despoil them of everything; but the events will play out differently.

Then, Habakkuk's text, follows a series of descriptions of the rebellious, the evil people who have built this parasitic supra-national empire and all their minions who live off their empire—the Globalist One-World-Government/One-World-Order. ... *A strong man's pride can fool him, but he will not find peace. He is like death—he always wants more and more. And, like death, he will never be satisfied. He will continue to defeat other nations and to make those people his prisoners.* I can see this all around me; can't you?

Isn't that exactly what we have witnessed for over two hundred years? There is no end to the rapacious controls and overreach these people demand, impose, threaten, and corrupt to get. It touches all the nations of the earth and every aspect of people's lives. It uses the most invasive and most powerful tools to accomplish their goals. Everyday, we think that we have reached the nadir of human decency, to find out that the reach of evil has metastasized into new directions and new depths. It could be depressing if we did not have Daniel and Habakkuk.

At this point, Habakkuk's text switches to the righteous side and how the defeat of the evil ones will be perceived by the good people: *But soon enough, all those* [good] *people will laugh at them and tell stories about their defeat. They will laugh and say, "it's too bad that the men who took so many things will not get to keep them! They made themselves rich by collecting debts".* Now that we are in the time of the end, justice is coming *"soon enough"*. And as Daniel tells us: it is divine justice. It will not be trifled with. And we should not feel contrived compassion for these people when God executes His plan.

A very apropos tidbit of information is offered here: *They made themselves rich by collecting debts.* Debt is the very enslaving process that the Globalists' elite have used for more than two centuries; this is how they gained their ascendency and secured their control. They have made kingdoms and nations their debtors—and leaving them no possibility for ever clearing those debts.

Proverb 22:7 says: *The borrower is a slave to the lender*, Romans 13:8 (J.B. Phillips) says: *Keep out of debt altogether*. This is not a suggestion; it is a command. The Globalist bankers targeted kings and governments to be the original debtors, understanding very well that kings and governments produce nothing at all; therefore, the populations living under these kings and governments would end up ruthlessly enslaved—through taxation—to eternally pay for the follies of their corruptible leaders (who control the militaries, which are their enforcers)... And the original culprits—kings and governments—would not be blamed! This is another uncanny detail that tells us that the text refers to the current Globalist One-World-Government.

> Note: Most of the original kings who were bought out and compromised by Global financiers claimed to be Christians. They had God's command to *Keep out of debt altogether;* had they obeyed, had they been faithful—had they denied themselves and submitted to God—they would have blessed their countries instead of selfishly selling their own people into economic slavery.

> Note: In our times, we—the "Christian" people—use casuistry to justify going into debt. For example, we exclude from this simple, clear command things like: houses, cars, businesses or schooling... We are wrong, dead wrong. We deserve what this brings us in return. For Jesus' followers, there is never a valid justification for borrowing.

Now we come to the part where Habakkuk lays out what the population victimized by the Globalists will do, what they can expect to do and should prepare to do. *Strong man* [evil cabal], *you have taken money from people. One day they will wake up and realize what is happening* [God's reckoning], *and they will stand against you. They will take things from you, and you will be very afraid. You have stolen things from many nations, so they will take much from you. You have killed many people and destroyed lands and cities. You have killed all the people there.* (And this has happened as Habakkuk foretold.)

One day, those who are looking up and watching the God of the universe, will see Him make His move and they will understand what is happening. They will be able to move in step with Him; to stand up and to despoil the tyrants of today as Jesus destroys them—small and big. They will be able to wrest out all these controls and riches and free the goods and the means. Again, Peter's words echo here: *It is most important for you to understand what will happen in the last days.*

In the wake of God's actions, the people who *are good* will *stand against* the predatory evil people of the Globalist One-World-Government and against their paid stooges and traitors in our midst—at all levels (Deep State). The good people will wake up, realize what has been happening and they will dig their heels in and rise up. (We hear the word: Great Awakening, a lot. It sure seems appropriate.)

So, it is God in Jesus, the *stone not cut by human hands*, who will utterly destroy this Satanic cabal (as clearly specified in Daniel 2) but, the good people must be awake and must be willing to stand against the Globalists and their paid minions everywhere. We have to turn loose all that had been bound. As we will see, believers must first be aware of what God is doing then stand so that they can loot their former predators and free the resources! The fighting is God's, the looting is human. 2 Chronicles 20:24 – 30 is a beautiful precedent for this principle.

The process of divine destruction of the fourth and final empire will not happen while we sleep; many people must be awake so that God may receive the glory brought by His actions. We have to make our stand—even though the actual fight is not ours. (We will demand and loosen the possessions of the people of this cabal. The spoils will be let loose... As mentioned above, it is the same process God had used for His people and against their enemies during Jehoshaphat's reign [2 Chronicles 20]) and even before that for the Hebrews in Egypt as regards their former enslavers.

In a classical divine poetic justice, the righteous will *take things from* them. God's people will get the spoils; they will loot these louts!

What is planned is not simply the cessation of the predatory and murderous activities and intents of the Globalist's One-World-Government by Divine action; it has a very human component: we are talking about the total ransacking of all the assets of the people who were doing the Globalists' bidding during our time. They kept amassing properties, riches, production centers and goods; but the righteous will take it all. Most of today's tyrants will lose their lives by God's hand, and many, many will lose everything else. We, the righteous, those "who listened" must accept this, and gear up for it. All the laws and controls that locked the elite's gains will have to be loosened and reversed; it takes foreknowledge and discernment to see what will need to happen.

As we have developed extensively in part one, the Globalist cabal have fomented wars incessantly—the endless wars. They have, as Habakkuk writes, *killed many people and destroyed lands and cities*. They have made sure that terrible destruction happened by financing both sides of every conflict they sponsored. As for our own country, unfortunately, many, many of our leaders, politicians, agencies, military brass and others in positions of power have thrown their lot with the ones God will destroy. So they will share their masters' fate. No pity or exemption will be given. And we should not extend our sympathies either. The loosening of unrighteous gains is not vengeance; it is a wrong righted. It is justice effected. Therefore, there will be a tremendous amount of loot to be gathered by the godly people. This fracture will affect families, communities, services and many other areas too numerous to mention here.

There will also be a functional vacuum created by this epic cleansing and extermination. Good people, followers of Jesus should be prepared to fill in where needed by demonstrating and sponsoring Godly solutions as well as proposing righteous limits to a now law-less and mandate-free population who may need direction.

The laws-and-mandates enforcing agencies, slaves to the fourth empire's system, will be discredited and toothless or even destroyed. And the framework of pervasive and ubiquitous laws and rules they made us live by will become obsolete and unenforcible. This overburdening of life by our current interweaving of rules and regulations—that only exist to shore up the greed-based system and to continue the rule of administrative petty tyrants—will make no sense anymore.

We will be free as we have never experienced in the length of our lives. But free means that we will have to take personal responsibility for our lives. It takes grit, initiative and courage to live free and most importantly to live as personally responsible, true human beings. This is another reason why true followers of Jesus must to be watchful and be prepared. If we are not, if we are indolently sleeping, or timid, then other people with crass motives will again fill in the voids and we will have only ourselves to blame.

Note: We will need a different breed of leaders. Leaders that do not need a pervasive system to function in—we need mental pioneers, courageous individuals who have demonstrated their grit at standing against the flow. People who encourage others, not people who want to control them. And that is where and when leaders with vision, biblical root and un-politicized spirit can make a difference: leaders who can think on their feet and are not awed by changing situations. Leaders who can see through the haze and the maze and point the way. Leaders who are givers; not takers. But we Christians must have our eyes open, our compass trued: we must be ready to move on; not to mill around like clueless cattle.

Finally: *You have killed all the people there.* How prescient God is: the Globalists embraced large scale eugenics, they pushed and imposed abortion, and population reduction not just in the USA, but in many countries. God said: go and multiply; they say: we must depopulate. God's punishing action will be the earned reckoning for this. The Globalists cabal have also killed millions in various poor countries by engineering deadly famines—in an age when the world could easily overproduce food of all kinds. This will be the reckoning for that as well.

And if we have trouble recognizing whom God is talking about, if we have trouble identifying the One-World-Order cabal and the corrupt elite of our countries, plus all the lower echelons who joined in (Deep State): God puts His laser pointer on them. *Look at you people! You get rich by cheating people and it hurts your own family!* Touché: they cheat. They spend their energies and our money to set in place all sorts of schemes to cheat and to exclude themselves from consequences. And, they don't give any consideration to whom they defraud. They cheat their own people: their countrymen, constituents, neighbors, even their families. Their global over-reach foists false fear and unnecessary burden on one and all; on their relatives as well as on the rest of us. Habakkuk is certainly rich in details, isn't he? Referring back to an item earlier in the text: Isn't getting rich while it hurt your own family exactly what the elite Hebraic component of this cabal did against their own brethren through the terrible extermination campaign of WWII that greatly enriched them?

You build your houses high on the cliff to protect yourself from danger. Can we see this? You bet, gated properties and elite communities, et al.

You planned shameful things, and that will bring shame to your own family. You have done wrong, and it will cost you your life. Over the last couple years, we have heard the phrase: "The Deep State people will not be able to walk down the streets". Well, there seems to be a lot of truth to that. From deliberate financial wrongdoings, to legal machinations, to peddling of influence, to sponsorship of wars, to pedophilia and human trafficking, their bag of shameful tricks is overflowing indeed. None of it has escaped God's notice. It will cost them their life.

It is worth repeating: This will not be the time for softhearted permissiveness and cheap slaps on the wrists. It is the time for judgment—divine judgment. We better side with the Judge! This is the end of the game for these people. They will go down with all their dear ones alongside them. The final price for many: It will cost them their lives. They callously robbed the quality of life of untold numbers and they took the lives of many more. The divine collector is coming by.

The description continues on the same vein. I will simply copy some of it here: *Look at them! They kill people to build their city and do wicked things to make their walled city strong. But the LORD All-Powerful has decided that a fire will destroy everything that those people worked to build. All their work will be for nothing. Then people everywhere will know about the Glory of the LORD. This news will spread just as water spreads out into the sea...*

This paragraph echoes Daniel 2. God's destruction will be unrelenting, and very public, like fire. All they ever worked for, all they ever corrupted to get, all the deals they made in dark rooms and all the defrauding of innocents...will be for nothing. Not only their ill-gotten gains will be nullified; but they will have to pay the penalties of their actions. The justice will be thorough.

And, the purpose and timing of it all is so that people everywhere will know about the Glory of the LORD—this is what it's about. This is God Almighty making Himself visible and known. God will do this very publicly and also in a very revealing way so that people will see HIM in it. He will not share His glory with "fate" or "accident" or "karma": He will get the glory for it all.

... They will know the LORD's anger... Evil ruler, you will drink from that cup. You will get shame, not honor... You hurt many... and stole much... So you will be afraid because of the people who died and because of the bad things you did to [individuals and countries]. *You will be afraid because of what you did to those cities and to the people who lived there...*

These people will know the LORD's anger: this is knowledge by experience. This is not simply information. They will know God's anger because they will experience it physically, mentally, spiritually—in full. For example: informatively, I "know" about the concentration camps in World War 2, from reading about it; but the people who were there know from the full experience of it. The people of the Globalists' Empire will know experientially the LORD's anger.

God will shine His spotlight on them; they will be revealed, He will peel back the layers of obfuscation. They will be uncovered—themselves and their deeds. The unblinking light of divine justice will glaringly expose the evil actors and their schemes. The good people will see how they have been robbed. How they have been defrauded and by whom. They will see by whom and for what they have been widowed.

And just as importantly, these evil actors will know that their victims now know! And worst of all: that their victims are now empowered. The breaking of the dams of pent up anger, frustrations, sorrows, misery and losses will be a very scary thing to witness. And God will not attenuate any part of it. Sobering, isn't it?

... *The sickness went before Him, and the destroyer followed behind Him. He stood and judged the earth*. Can we recall the plagues God used to bring about the first exodus? What plagues will precede and pave the way for the second exodus in our time during the destruction of this evil regime? We do not know yet; but we will soon see. We can all remember the Bible texts about the first exodus and we can rejoice for the fact that God's people were spared then. This is very good to know: the divine battering will not affect the righteous people.

In Moses' time, the Egyptians—who opposed God and had preyed upon His people—were destroyed or terminally ruined. And, God's people left with the loot. They asked for the Egyptians riches and these were given to them. Food for thought, don't you think?

Then people everywhere will know about the Glory of the LORD. This is very important because it resonates with many passages that deal with this specific series of events. These events are what I call God's march of glory, because, in every passage that deals with any part of it, God always says: "and all the people will see Me and what I do... all the people will know about Me" (paraphrased)... As mentioned in part one and developed in the book *Revelation the Fair God*, God's march of glory begins with the destruction of the fourth empire. It segues into the divinely powered and led second exodus of the Hebrews from every country, then the battle of Gog and Magog follows, in turn, that ushers the seven years of blessings in Israel and finally God will conduct the rapture of the saints. God will receive His full glory at, and through, each of these steps.

Chapter 3:13 – 15, Habakkuk brings to remembrance the first exodus of the Hebrews. The reference is interesting because throughout part one, I elaborated on the timing of destruction of the Globalists' Empire and the scouring of the population. I proposed that it would precede and be related to the second exodus of the Hebrew people out of every country of the world. It is interesting that Habakkuk should also tie with it by association. His written words clearly had no meaning in the time of Habakkuk's writing because there was no punishing duress exercised by God on the Chaldeans of antiquity. There was no culling of His returning people with the destruction of the unfaithful. Nor was there a divinely organized and dramatically led by God exodus out of the Babylon captivity of antiquity.

But as abundantly prophesied, all these aspects will be present for the second exodus in our days ... As God said: Just as I did in Egypt...

Habakkuk 3: the pep talk

Habakkuk 3:17 – 19 is interesting for us as well. It tells us that even though we do not yet see the fruits (figs and olive are not on the trees yet) we should resolutely set our eyes on YHWH/Jesus. And that is not all: while doing this focusing, we should already rejoice and be glad in Him—"in God my Savior."

This passage tells me that even though it looks like the evil people of the fourth empire still have the ascendance, I should shift my focus to my God. I should act, talk and think according to the bedrock of the promise of His words in Daniel 2 and Habakkuk 2. I should move on beyond the appearances and set myself to expecting God's upcoming magnificent deeds. The deeds will be there as surely as the morning always comes—regardless of the state of humanity or the season of life.

God says He will do it; so He will.

This brings us to a most important item: the expected role of the follower of the new and permanent Master: Jesus.

The role of God's people through of the destruction of the cabal

The society in which we live has myriads of laws, countless agencies' mandates and regulations, thousands of them arcane, most of them crafted for the sole purpose of increasing government control over us, to rigidly haze us through the business of living each day. They are pervasive and they touch every detail of life. We automatically comply because we have been herded to do so since we were born. A lot of these laws preceded us. The initiators of our country had put up a valiant effort to change the idea of government and empower God's creature: the person. But before long, politicians and foreign actors had plugged all the holes that permitted the light of freedom to be enjoyed by all.

Most of our laws are enacted by politicians and administered by unelected officials, both of whom are in the employ of the Globalist's One-World-Government masters—to benefit themselves first and always, to perpetuate their privileges. These agencies' rules, their laws and mandates do not serve normal human functions; they only serve governmental functions. When all these corrupt and compromised governments fall; all these laws, mandates and rules will be useless. There will be an incredible breath of fresh air, a new dynamism. Followers of Jesus should be ready to promote Godly principles, principles created for humans with their God-given free will. We should be ready to promote freedom and demonstrate its reality.

Beginning with the Babylonian Empire of old, each supra-national empire left traces—even skeletons—of their power and control mechanisms. Each borrowed from the previous. People in every generation have studied these and distilled their principles in order to duplicate them in their time. Today, we have vestiges of the first three supra-national empires in use for controlling our lives.This is why God explained through Daniel that when the "Stone" hits the feet of iron and clay, He will obliterate and blow away, make disappear, any trace of all four of these empires. There will be nothing left of those human constructs that could be put to coercive use again. Warning: this does not mean that evil will be absent; it will be present (we are not in the 1,000 year reign) but the structure of government will not be what those empires were and still are.

When the "Stone" vaporizes all the supra-national empires, not a trace of them will be left. That means none of their legacies will exist or apply.

So, how is a person to live when this happens? Most people living then will not know how to live. The sudden freedom from all these unnecessary, politically motivated, shackles will be bewildering. Fresh directions will be needed. We don't want to slide back into the tyranny of making rules just for their own sake. A few, true life-enhancing principles must be carefully proposed to replace the tens of thousands of rules and regulations that have boxed us in, every days. This is when the followers of the "Stone"—Jesus—will have a role to play. They will have practiced the ability to stand alone for what is right, to be responsible to God and before man; so they will have what it takes. And they will be able to pass it on. Also, they will be able to do so because they know Him who now sets the tone, they understand Him thus will be able to apply His principles and advise others. He made us; He knows how we can best operate.

The sudden disappearance of the mind-controlling framework will affect every aspect of life. Here is a few examples from our recent history that will shed some light on this.

Medicine for example: Since the early 1,900s the practice of medicine and the teaching of medicine have been altered by the globalist agenda, beginning with the Rockefeller family's forceful encroachment. Medicine, before then, was an adaptive and diversified art; there were many independent schools of Medicine... And strange as it may seem, real progresses were being made. Good and bad ideas were being debated, put to the test of reality. Left alone medicine would have continued to make steady progress. But it became "sponsored" thus controlled, enslaved to an agenda. And today we do not have this natural expression of medicine; we have corporate medicine—a monolithic, top-to-bottom structure where doctors simply apply what they are paid to kowtow to.

Medicine has only progressed according to corporate priorities and profits. You see: healing does not pay; treating sicknesses and symptoms does. So promoting healthy and natural solutions is not corporately motivating; whereas ignoring healing and combating sicknesses by developing batteries of expensive drugs or procedures (each new one more expensive that the one it replaces) is very profitable for the pharmaco/medical complex. Medical schools teach what their generous grants pay them to propagate. Recently, we had a draconian push for total control by vaccination, health passports, etc. This types of events could be absent in life post-fourth empire. The true believers input will help this happen.

The pursuit of health at the personal and corporate level has been skewered toward the exclusive reliance on expensive drugs that require a full retinue of peripheral drugs to shield harmful side effects, which in turn require a third tier of expensive drugs to shield these secondary drugs' side effects, etc. And the populations everywhere have become weaker, sicker and generally unhealthy. Life expectancy in America is dropping; not increasing. The process of healing has been forgotten, replaced by the short-sighted—and often deadly—pursuit of instantaneous masking of symptoms. If the symptoms disappear, the disease must have been vanquished, right? We do not treat the roots of problems, we simply cover up their superficial expressions. The medico/pharmaceutical behemoth has become omnipotent and tyrannical. It does not permit any dissent. We even invented a term to refer to the state of life today: co-morbidity. Imagine that! The ruination of the population's health was actually one of the avowed aim of the fourth empire.

Healing is a process—often a long process. Symptom masking is instantaneous—or at least very rapid; it is an easy sell. The industry has substituted what was good for what is quick and easy—but highly profitable. They have built the people's expectations around this. "Look: no more pain; no more problem!" As a result the general population is far less healthy than it was a hundred years ago.

Simple health principles were systematically turned around by politically and greed motivated actors. Sugar, the world killer was elevated to the status of savior while health promoting fats were vilified and made to be public enemy number one. It will not be easy for people to step out of these adopted premises into a brand new world where these false counsels are not enforced or forced-advertised anymore.

All other areas of life will be affected. Staying with nutrition for example: How will we eat when the Globalists' undeclared additives will neither be hidden nor deemed necessary anymore? Take owning or operating a car, an airplane; the legal operation of these vehicles will be different without the overbearing, all-intrusive reach of the Deep State. Take education: Schools and schooling, freed from their satanic overlords will also be a different proposition. What will happen to the potential of the young when the institutional mind numbing Department of Education is not there anymore? When practicality and effectiveness will be the goal? What a breath of fresh air it will bring.

And the "Stone"—Jesus—will not go away. He will not fade in the background. He will be the only supra-national basis of power, because He will be whom everyone will talk about. Those who know Him truly and have followed Him will become invaluable then. Believers, we must be ready to follow Jesus, prepared to fill our role then.

At creation, God gave rights and directions that define our humanity. We have surrendered so many of these individual, inherent, creational rights and individual responsibilities to the supra-national empires, and to the Globalists' in particular, that we are now clueless about what we can naturally do or cannot do, what we can think or cannot think, and what we can say or cannot say. I have read somewhere that it is impossible for an average, well-meaning American to wake up in the morning and live an honest day without breaking a slew of laws and regulations. Again: those who know and follow the Maker have a role to play for humanity when these abnormal controls are taken off. When the cages open up.

Here is a picture for example: consider the Chinese foot-binding customs and rules. It took people who were free from the foot-binding legacy—read missionaries—to guide the process of exiting that tyranny. Disciples of Jesus should be free by definition and thus the best to promote and exemplify a free life.

God/Jesus is in control, in total control. Things are playing out exactly as he foretold 2,500 years ago. It is His playbook. Believers: wake up and sing His praises. The stone is about to hit the feet of iron mixed with clay.

Jeremiah 50 – 51 (ERV)

This is an interesting synergetic passage to the contents of this presentation. As the reader proceeds through these chapters, he builds an understanding that "Babylon" could be a type of kingdom; not just the Babylon of antiquity.

Jeremiah 50 is interesting to me because the prophet writes about what happens to Babylon and the Jews from the turbulent era just before the defeat of Judea and the ensuing exile in Babylon. We naturally assume that through his given prophecies he only covers events of antiquity; but then we come to a passage like this one where actual antiquity has not played out according to Jeremiah's scenarios.

So was Jeremiah a false prophet? But if he was, then why would he remain enshrined in the hall of fame of Hebrew prophets? ... Or, was he laying out events for a future time, a different Babylon?

I would like to take the passage in the order it is written. Verse 20 *The LORD says, "At that time people will try hard to find Israel's guilt, but there will be no guilt. People will try to find Judah's sins, but no sins will be found. That is because I am saving a few survivors from Israel and Judah. And I am forgiving them for all their sins."*

In this verse we find the arguments, that place the prophesied actions outside the Babylonian captivity and around exodus 2.0:

First, at the end of the Babylonian captivity of antiquity, Israel's guilt was not wiped out. Neither Israel's sins nor Judah's were voided. Forgiveness of sin came centuries later: Matthew 1:21 says *You will call him Jesus. Give him that name because he will save his people for their sins* (ERV) And the en-masse joining of the Hebrew people into Jesus' covenant is still in the future (it will happen for exodus 2.0).

At the end of the Babylonian exile, God did not save a few people from the northern tribes of Israel: Israel's guilt remained even though these tribes were absent from the biblical scene. These northern tribes had already exited recorded history; the Bible had stopped tracking them. They had been scattered to the four winds. And to this day, we, mortals, do not know who they are among us. Only God knows.

So, this oddly timed verse fits perfectly with exodus 2.0 that will follow the destruction of the fourth Babylon-type kingdom—the destruction of the Globalists' supra-national empire. And Jesus will indeed save a few from both Israel (10 northern tribes) and Judah (Judah and Benjamin). They are the ones who will accept his everlasting covenant when they pass under his rod. (The others, the rebellious ones, the covenant deniers, will be destroyed and will never see the land of Israel again.)

Verses 23 – 25 *"Babylon was called the 'hammer of the whole earth'. But now the hammer is shattered."* *The hammer of the whole earth* is a perfect fit with the fourth empire described by Daniel 2:40: *"That kingdom will be strong like iron* [the material hammers are made of]. *Just like iron breaks things and smashes them to pieces, that fourth kingdom will break all the others kingdoms and smash them to pieces.* That's what a hammer does.

Now the hammer is shattered, this part of the verse corresponds exactly to Daniel 2:34: *The rock* [Jesus] *hit the statue on its feet of iron and clay and smashed them.* The striking head of a hammer is made of iron and the iron will be shattered by Jesus.

It fascinates me that Jeremiah's prophecy precedes Daniel's vision for Nebuchadnezzar's dream. Yet, as with the entire bible, scripture is faithfully continuous; there are no dissonances. The only difference is that Jeremiah thought he was talking about Babylon, and Daniel was given the rest of the context.

In between the last two verses, we read verse 24: *Babylon, I set a trap for you, and you were caught before you knew it. You fought against the LORD, so you were found and captured.* This is not the Babylon of the Nebuchadnezzars. The Babylon of antiquity was blessed into being by God: *The God of heaven has given you a kingdom, power, strength and glory. He has given you control, and you rule over people... God has made you a ruler over them all...* (Daniel 2:37). The Babylon of antiquity did not fight against the LORD. Does this seem like God was setting a trap to trip the Babylon of Nebuchadnezzar?

In actuality, Babylon of antiquity was where God chose to send the "good figs" of Judah. Jeremiah, himself had written: *This is what the Lord, the God of Israel, says: The good figs represent the exiles I sent from Judah to the land of the Babylonians. I will watch over and care for them, and I will bring them back here again. I will build them up and not tear them down. I will plant them and not uproot them. I will give them hearts that recognize me as the Lord.*

The LORD expands on this topic later (Jeremiah 29:4 – 7) *This is what the Lord of Heaven's Armies, the God of Israel, says to all the captives he has exiled to Babylon from Jerusalem: "Build homes, and plan to stay. Plant gardens, and eat the food they produce. Marry and have children. Then find spouses for them so that you may have many grandchildren. Multiply! Do not dwindle away! And work for the peace and prosperity of the city where I sent you into exile* [Babylon]. *Pray to the Lord for it, for its welfare will determine your welfare".* Does this sound antagonistic toward Babylon?

Once the Jews were in Babylon, albeit, after the horrible ordeal of the vanquishing battles they were subjected to, they were not grossly mistreated. From my vantage point, the old Babylon did not seem more sinful than its captive Judah. It actually proved to be neither better nor worse. Like Judah, it followed idols, but when corrected, it enthroned the God of heaven and the seesawing between idolatry and godliness went back and forth with each succeeding monarch.

However, the Babylon of today—the fourth empire of the Globalist cabal—is, and always was, a kingdom of Satanists/Luciferians who have systematically opposed God. It is a cabal that has warred against all facets of righteousness and godliness. There were never times in the last two and a-half centuries when the Globalists repented and enthroned the God of Heaven and earth. The Globalists have relentlessly *"fought against the LORD"* as Jeremiah writes. And they have sought to destroy Jesus' followers wherever they could. They do not seesaw between redeeming periods and hellbent episodes. They worship Satan and fight against the good—always and everywhere.

So, verse 24 aptly speaks of today's supra-national empire of the Globalists.

Back to verse 25, *"The LORD has opened up His storeroom and brought out the weapons of His anger. The LORD God All-powerful brought out those weapons because He has work to do in the land of the Chaldeans."*

Again, this does not fit with the Babylon of antiquity. It does not reflect the events of the end of the Babylonian Empire. At that time, it was the Medes, not God, who took over from the Chaldeans. But here, verse 25 tells us that God will use His own weapons *because He has work to do...* Daniel tell us that the weapon is Jesus, the Stone. In antiquity, God did not do any particular thing in the land of the Chaldeans at the fall of the Nehuchadnezzars. He did not reveal Himself there and did not get the glory... But He will this time.

Verses 26 and 27 echo the thorough grinding, the methodical killing that will take place when God demolishes the fourth empire; it is not representative of what happened when the power passed from the Chaldeans to the Medes then to the Persians in Daniel's time.

Verse 28, "*People are running out of Babylon. They are escaping from that country* [system] *and coming to Zion. They are telling everyone the good news about what the LORD is doing. The LORD our God is giving Babylon the punishment it deserves.*"

In antiquity, at the end of their captivity, the Jews did not run out of Babylon. They had passed from the control of the Chaldeans to that of the Medes then to Persians without any recorded duress—at least not that I could find. Later, they were set free by their new masters: the Medes, then the Persians and encouraged to go back to their country and rebuild. And those who went are not recorded as having "run away"... And the kingdom they left was not visited by God's anger. Actually the record shows that Cyrus, Darius and Artaxerxes—representative of each of the succeeding power changes—were rather good to the Hebrews and respectful of the God of heaven.

So again, with verse 28, God is talking about the modern supra-national system, the fourth empire. The progression of the verse is perfect: God destroys the fourth empire, identifies, judges and moves His ancient people to Zion. "Run from Babylon" is an interesting phrase because, that is exactly the choice Jesus will present the Hebrews: escape your fate now, run away and choose Me. Why the urgency? Because it will be a matter of life or death. God will destroy this Babylon and kill every Hebrew who belongs to the Globalist's cabal and sides against Jesus. So, He exhorts them to have a change of heart and flee their affiliation to it. Today, I seem to see many Jews deeply entrenched into the Globalist's plot. Some hold very high ranks in it... So the warning and the urging are à propos.

Again, in verse 28, we find the direct segueing from the destruction of the One-World-Government clique into exodus 2.0.

Finally, we can read that the people that God moves to the land of Israel—not to the State of Israel—will see God's action and will witness and attest to His deeds to their Israeli brethren.

Verse 29b, *"Babylon did not respect the LORD. Babylon was very rude to the Holy One of Israel."* This does not fit well with the Babylon of the Nebuchadnezzars. Indeed, that Babylon made great declarations of faith at times (Daniel 3, 4, 6). Of course it fell back into idolatry each time; but so did God's Jewish people.

On the other hand, the Babylon of today has systematically, willfully and strenuously disrespected YHWH and has gone out of its way to be rude to the God of the Bible. Consider all the Satanic symbolisms, the statues of Moloch cropping up everywhere, the absolutely blasphemous artwork these people sponsor...the promotion and protection of abortion, homosexuality, transgenderism, pedophilia...all provocative abominations.

Verse 34, *"This is what the LORD All-powerful says... [He]* will get them back... He will defend them strongly. He will argue their case so that He can let their land rest."* This verse sheds the same light: the scriptures had said that the Jews (the two southern tribes) who returned from the Babylonian captivity would *rebuild... but in times of trouble and unrest;* not in a time of rest (Daniel 9:25). And history verifies this. So verse 34 here does not apply to the end of the Babylonian captivity of antiquity. In our time, at the outset of exodus 2.0, they will experience rest—a rest no one will be able to threaten.

The text here tells us is that Israel, when it returns in our time, will be defended by God and the land will have rest—which is exactly what Ezekiel 38 and 39 prophecy. After exodus 2.0, even the Gog and Magog war will not bring the battle to the people of Israel: Israel will not fire a shot. God will take care of the entire affair. God will bring the belligerents near Israel, and when they decide to attack, God will crush them in many ways... to the very last combatant.

So, again, Jeremiah's text is referring to exodus 2.0, and to the time that includes and follows Gog and Magog.

Verse 46, "*Babylon will fall, and that fall will shake the earth*" When the Medes took over Babylon, there was continuity. Life in former Chaldean Babylon went on—only the regime changed. When the Medes then the Assyrians went down, their falls did not "shake the earth".

In contrast, in our times, the Globalists' supra-national dictatorship will be abruptly terminated, vaporized. And since it is deeply embedded in every nation on earth, in every society and even in most families; its fall will indeed shake the earth.

Verse 46 continues: "*People in all the nations will hear about the destruction of Babylon.*" When Babylon of antiquity lost to the Medes, then the Medes to the Assyrians and these to the Greeks I doubt that every people living in Western Europe, Northern Europe, Mid and Southern Africa, Japan or the American landmass heard about the defeat of the Chaldeans.

But in our time, every single person living that day will see the destruction of our current Babylon. They will probably watch the process live on their phones, tablets, computers and TV screens.

In our time, when Jesus, the *stone*, divinely destroys the fourth empire and its minions His true followers will not suffer through the process either. We will come through safely. This seems to be a biblical model: during Noah's time, God's faithful followers (eight in all) did not suffer as God destroyed all guilty men and most living things and reshaped the earth. His followers were marvelously insulated from it all in a special ark. They did not flee: they walked into the safe haven of the ark and God closed the door behind them—shepherded all the way.

<u>Note</u>: Jeremiah's text alludes to a kingdom of the North as a tool God would send and use to destroy this "Babylon". Could the destruction have a human component to it? Which country today could be that kingdom of the North? We'll just have to see... But America does not fit this possibility.

<u>One further note</u>: Those who come through the destruction of the fourth empire—believers as well as non-believers—won't carry all the artifices of today's "successful" life with them. Those artifices were the assets that the Globalists urged people to desire, to amass, to fight for, to strive to get. It was the influence that was thought necessary to progress successfully within the evil empire's system... all these will be made irrelevant and useless. So, just like Noah and his sons, we may begin a different life, in a different paradigm. As Daniel 2 says: the stone does not go away; its effect endures universally. Yet, greed will remain and people will be people; so things will not be perfect, yet the change will be dramatic.

Life after the destruction of the fourth empire

Things will be different

It would not do to leave this exposé here and omit to delve into the spiritual war that will follow the destruction of this fourth empire. So, once the fourth empire is crushed and even deleted from history; what format will the struggle between good and evil take? What will happen everywhere and in the United States in particular? As Daniel 2 tells us, the stone-not-cut-by-human-hands will remain and grow to dominate; no other form of world-wide, supra-national government will ascend; but then, how will this work out, since sin will still be present and the deceiver still active?

Isaiah 64:1 – 2 introduces a rhetorical scenario: *If you would tear open the skies and come down to earth, then everything will change. Mountains would melt before You. The mountains would burst into flames like burning bushes. The mountains would boil like water on the fire. Then your enemies would learn about you. And all the nations would shake with fear when they see* you. What if this would happen? Wouldn't they indeed?

Having set the concept up, Isaiah 64:3 lets us know that this scenario is what will happen: *But you have done awesome things that we did not expect. You came down, and mountains shook in fear before you.* The Rock will strike!

We will enter a different world paradigm. We cannot conceive "life then" by "life now". Indeed revolutionary events will have happened: Jesus will have revealed Himself, personally, magisterially and effectively to all.

- The Bible says that every human will clearly see Him destroy of the fourth empire, the supra-national system they had all lived under. Everyone will see that the most powerful empire, the most destructive empire in history is no match at all for Jesus, the God of the Bible. So, number one: everyone will know that man is no match for God.

- The Bible also tells us that every human being will see Jesus carry out the terrible judgment of the rebelling Hebrews, in every country where they currently live.

- Also, the Bible tells us that everyone in the world will see Jesus very publicly and majestically move the remnant of Jacob's descendants to Israel—every single one of those who embraced Jesus' covenant. Everyone will be clearly aware that the true God is the God of the Bible, the God of Jacob. So, number two: Everyone will know that the God who acts is the God of the Hebrews.

- The Bible tells us that every person of all the nations will see Jesus' action through the absolute demolition of all the false gods at Gog and Magog where the most widely recognized false god is destroyed—proven to be a human construct. Everyone will find out that all the gods are not gods at all: Jesus vanquished them. So, number three: Everyone will know that there are no alternatives to Jesus.

- In short order, every living person will have seen God in action, will have seen His identity: the God of Jacob, the God of the Bible. And will have seen that all other gods are only pretend gods: the only God is the God of the Bible, the God of Israel.

- And from Daniel 2, we can deduce that everyone, everywhere will be aware that Jesus [the stone] rules the whole earth. He will not leave the scene.

Isaiah 64:4 – 5 finishes: *No one has ever heard of such a God. No one has ever heard such a story. No one has ever seen any God except you, who does such great things for those who trust him...* And then, they will have. This will be a novel era.

There has never been such a divine revealing and there has never been such a time in history as what the world will be like then. The world will have seen God. So, the universal question facing everyone will be: this is God, the only God; what are you personally going to do about it?

One of the aspect of the rock remaining and growing to fill the earth could be that after the above awe-inspiring acts of God, Jesus will now be and remain on the minds and on the inquiring lips of the now awaken world population. And this will last until the harvest is complete...some seven years later.

In a way, there will be two humanities: the descendants of Jacob, all surviving Hebrews vouched for by Jesus and joyfully getting to know him in Israel for at least seven years after Gog and Magog, and on the other side, outside the greater land of Israel: the Gentiles. The Gentiles are a step behind in time: God deals first with His ancient people.

Now, the Gentiles having actually seen Jesus in action will have the opportunity to join Him. This is why I have labelled this phase: the Great Harvest. People will seek the Jesus they have seen. Some will do so with an earnest and submissive heart; but others will look for ways to get what they selfishly want while embracing enough of Jesus to claim "membership". They will look for a "workaround"—to be able to claim Jesus; but on their own terms.

Everyone will seek the answer. Some will embrace the truth; some will be lured by the mirror of false Christianity; they will choose the mirror to further their own agendas.

In recap: The seven years that follow Gog and Magog are the time of the great harvest:

- When all the Hebrews, having embraced Jesus as the only divine covenant will come to know Him—as Ezekiel makes clear.

- With the deducible reciprocal that all the Gentiles will be sorted out: those who choose Jesus and surrender to Him (the great harvest of souls) and those who wanting their own way will eventually resolve to hate Him by the bias of the false Christianity.

A quick parenthesis

Before going into the above subject, let us dispatch an erroneous theory that keeps popping up. Over the centuries, much speculation and many lines have been written that propose that the fourth empire would be the kingdom of the antichrist—when the antichrist rules. (The time of what we usually call the great tribulations.) No; the ascendency of that ruler (antichrist) is not the fourth empire (no matter how evil the fourth empire may get to be). Because Daniel tells us that the fourth empire is a divided kingdom. The antichrist kingdom will not be a divided kingdom: *and all who live on earth will worship the beast* (Revelation 13:8).

So, as to the antichrist; this is how it will work out:

- At the rapture, God will hand over the remaining population to Satan and his antichrist-to-be. The people then will be on their own; "let those who are going to be killed be killed..."[Revelation 13:10) God will not be available to them throughout this process! The entire Gentile population left on earth at the rapture will begin the tribulations as individuals whose hearts are against the true God, against the biblical Jesus. It is <u>not</u> a spiritually divided population. They will all welcome the antichrist (the false Jesus). He will seem to vindicate their anti-Jesus choice and preferences.

- But, people argue: some will refuse the mark at the last moment. True, but that is not "division". As soon as such a person differs from the diktat of the antichrist—by refusing the mark—he or she is killed (beheaded). There will be no built-in opposition, no organized division, no divisive movement within the populace! The rider of the red horse (messenger) makes it clear that the overwhelming urge of the people will be to kill one another—not to group, associate or organize for the good. Only a few, lone individuals, here and there, will balk at committing their eternity to Satan and they will refuse the mark.

- Those who are not beheaded but <u>remain alive</u> after the rapture are all unrepentant; they form a single bloc of anti-Jesus mankind... (And the beheaded will not be part of the population anymore; so there is no division there). The kingdom of the antichrist is not a divided kingdom. The individuals will have no affinity one toward another—as the red horse of the apocalypse tells us—but the regime, the kingdom will not be divided.

Therefore, as already mentioned above, we can aver that Daniel's fourth empire is not the reign of the antichrist.

Now, back to the text.

The spiritual battle field

Between Gog and Magog and the rapture of the believers, during that incredibly momentous stretch of seven years of history, a tremendous battle will take place for the fate of the Gentile souls everywhere. (The Hebrews are not part of this, Ezekiel tells us that they will <u>all</u> come to Jesus their Messiah and get to know Him in Israel during this seven+ year hiatus.)

The battle that will take place outside Israel for the Gentiles' souls will be conducted under a totally novel premise: It will be a battle between real Christianity and false Christianity. It will <u>not</u> be between Yahweh/Jesus and Allah or Baal or any other deity and it will not be between Yahweh/Jesus and no god at all; because every body will have understood the reality of the God of the Bible.

So, Satan will switch to a game of mirrors, he will present his false Christianity as the only medium to the Jesus—the God they have seen. This is the false Christianity Satan has been nurturing and evolving for centuries for such a time as this.

As outlined above, the entire Gentile population of the world (the non-Hebrews) will be keenly aware of Jesus/God and they will then want to know about the God they saw in action. Some will reject Him outright and refuse to have anything to do with Him. They will be easy recruits for the false Jesus. But the others, those drawn to Him will not be able to discount Him outright anymore or pretend that He does not exist—as they can do now—because they will have seen Him. However, most of them will not "know" Him. They will want to know more about the awesome God they saw.

So, who will vie to present Him? To make Him known? Who will *"make followers of all people in the world... baptize them... teach them to obey everything Jesus has taught"*?

On God's side, it will be His true followers. But on Satan's side, who will the evil one present as Jesus' adversary? He will not be able to float he narrative that the God of the Bible does not exist—because Jesus will be the One God everybody will want to know about. So, Satan will push his "Most Christian", his "Only True Christianity": the religion he invented and groomed for centuries for this purpose. He will use the mirror of the false religion that claims to be Christian, that claims to be the only way to Jesus, and to be the only dispenser of God's power and grace: the Roman Catholic Church.

So the battle will be between the true Gospel and the false gospel. Between biblical truth of biblical Christianity and the mirror games of false Christianity as embodied by the Roman Church. What happens during the seven+ years after Gog and Magog is the fulfillment of the parable of the wheat and the tares of Matthew 13. The tares in the parable are understood to be darnel. A useless grass that look a lot like wheat; but is not. When it first sprouts and begins to grow it is very difficult to tell it apart from the wheat.

Jesus planted the true seed, the good seed—the good news. The apostles passed it on and disseminated it to us all. And, full of promises, a crop of righteous believers began to grow and spread. Then Satan planted a false crop, a non-digestible, useless crop in that ground that had been prepared for the good crop. It is a copy cat, disconnected to the source and alien to the true seed's destiny. It grew unmolested because it "looked" like the real thing.

Within a few centuries after the good news was planted the false wheat began to appear and has grown ever since. It has striven to crowd out, choke out the good seed. And as per the parable, God did not remove the false religion at its inception—as Jesus explains in Matthew 13—He has allowed it to grow alongside the good crop: His crop. The good crop is the control crop, all final events are timed on the condition and ripening of the good crop. The spiritual false crop—the darnel of the parable—is immaterial to God's plan. In the parable, the field's owner instructs his workers not to pull up the darnel, because it looks just like the wheat so, unawares, they may damage the good stuff. Some of the stuff they identify as darnel may yet prove to be good wheat. The Roman Catholic behemoth does everything, says everything necessary to be like the good news...but it is not.

When the good crop reaches its fullness; the harvest will be taken into the Master's barn (rapture) and then, only then, the worthless false crop will be cut and burned. But even then, God will make sure that any glossed over wheat grain is picked up. God is thorough, the good harvest will be followed by the very methodical gleaning of individual kernels who turn out to be wheat and not darnel (This is why the Tribulation is called "the time of testing" in Revelation 3).

So, the evil, false crop has been allowed to remain and grow through the centuries, it has relentlessly attempted to choke (kill) the good crop. It has lured seekers with its polished mirror. It will be allowed to remain alongside the true crop all the way until the rapture. The most potent and prevalent false crop planted by Satan is the Roman Catholic Church. From the outside, it looks like the real thing, it affirms not only to be the right thing; but it also proclaims to be the only true universal church. It claims to be the only path to Jesus and to hold the exclusive control key to paradise. The Roman Catholic Church has built on these assertions all through the centuries.

Note: Religions like Islam will be immaterial in the post-Gog and Magog hiatus because they and their gods will have been glaringly exposed, thus made irrelevant. Sincere people, having seen Jesus in action will want to know about Him and no other; the trap for these people will be the forgery that pretends to be Christ's own. It will be the same with the hybrid types of false religions like Mormonism which, like Islam, have a different Jesus and a different God (according to them, Jesus is the blood brother of Satan and God-the-Father was once a man) and also, like the Roman Church, the Mormon Church insists that it is the only path to the god of redemption, the only gate to gleeful eternity.

These other make-believe Christian religions are only distractions, the largest and most powerful agent of the false, the imitation Christianity has been—and will be—the Roman Catholic Church. Jesus lays this out clearly in Chapters 17 of Revelation. And during the reign of the antichrist, the Roman Catholic Church will be the universal one-world-church. It will have limitless, universal powers to suppress and kill—skills it has practiced punctually over the centuries. If you are a true Christian; do not fear it: you won't be there.

The Roman Catholic Church emerged and grew as a false religion pretending to be the one and only true church of Christianity (read Dave Hunt's *A Woman Rides the Beast* or read the relevant chapters of *Revelation the Fair God*). It claims to be:

- The only access to the God of the Bible and its only mediator.

- The only advocate controlling the transitioning of the souls into Heaven.

- The only Advocate/Redeemer of the souls in Hell—or in Purgatory as their mythology outlines.

- Its worldwide leader, the Pope is the Vicar of Christ; which means: the Christ-substitute (we cannot make the stuff up)!

The seven years' time of the great harvest will be the clash of the Gospels—the Good News and the kinked Catholic gospel to Hell. However, for that duration, Jesus will be the overall, supra-national power; not the Roman Catholic Church. Therefore, the Catholic Church's capability and propensity for killing and destruction will be kept in check. This is a time when Jesus/God rejoices, the time of <u>His</u> harvest, a time of celebration, not of mourning. The false church will not be able to just wantonly kill the true believers because it will not control the field. Just like in the parable of the wheat and the darnel, it will be the Master's harvesters who will accomplish the good harvest.

Later, God's restrictions will be lifted, and the Catholic Church—or I should say the now Universal-One-Church—will again be able to kill and destroy during the antichrist's reign (as it had in the various countries where it was the state religion). We have an ancient precedent: Satan's power was kept in check in the garden of Eden before man surrendered his soul to him and ventured to dethrone God. Then death appeared.

The Roman Catholic Church has prepared the terrain for this particular time: in recent decades it has framed the narrative in preparation for what is coming. After warring against them for centuries; it is now wooing both the Moslems and the Evangelical Christians. Satan, the Vatican's master, knew what the coming fight would be about.

Satan knew that the Muslims (1.6 B plus) would be left without a god and would be grasping for a connection with the true God they would have seen in action. So, lately, through Rome, Satan has been courting the Muslims, preparing the narrative.

After centuries of deadly opposition to Islam, the infallible Roman Catholic Church did a U-turn. Popes now insist that Muslims and Catholics serve and worship the same god. And at least two popes have prayed in Muslim holy sites to affirm the point. After Gog and Magog, the Roman Catholic Church can then simply extend its deadly invitation to the lost or grieving Muslims: "Come to us, we are very big and very powerful, we are everywhere. Governments have kneeled before us everywhere for centuries... We are the only access to the god you had served before; you just had the wrong medium, the wrong venue. We are the only church of the God of the Bible, the God you saw. Come home!" It will be a powerful deception... and it is firmly in place today; ready to roll out!

The Roman Catholic Church has not limited its outreach to Muslims; it has extended variations of the theme toward Evangelical Christians and Charismatic Christians as well as old time protestant confessions—that is: any and all who call themselves Christian but are not building their faith and practices on the word of God only. The Roman Catholic Church has had quite an effect on the unmoored, the biblically weak, the TV centered "Christians". It has sappily played on their emotions: you must be nice. Nice trumps right. (This coming from the very tormentor who used to burn protestants at the stake!) And yellow-livered, effeminate protestant preachers and pastors have abounded in the direction the Roman Catholic Church has pointed. Spiritually shallow congregations are charmed: "be nice" rings well...

To be spared by God, these ungrounded Christian, or rebellious Christians, will have to choose to reject their counterfeit "ecumenical religions" and embrace the true Gospel. Or by closing their ears and eyes and continuing to cater to their druthers, they will amble along to Hell under the charms of the liar who has them more than half-convinced already. Their decision today is existential.

The Roman Catholic Church is gearing toward its final role: to be the One-World-Church of the time of the antichrist. So, besides the Muslims and the Evangelical Christians; it has made ecumenical overtures toward any and all religions. Decades ago, Pope Paul VI began the process by blessing the Second World Conference on Religion and Peace in Louvain (Belgium) where Buddhists, Christians, Confucianists, Hindus, Jains, Jews, Muslims, Shintoists, Sikhs, Zoroastrians and others sought to listen to the spirit within. Popes John XXIII then Paul VI had also joined with the Dalai Lama, and some Muslim and Buddhist leaders to work on the United Nations of religion. Pope John-Paul II forged on ahead with those agendas, so did his successors. Can you see the pattern? The poor godless (literally) people will be wooed with the message of the "only true church", the universal church, the entity that has been so nice to them in recent past...

> <u>Note</u>: Do I mean that every Roman Catholic today is doomed in this process? No, only those who will chose to remain within the bosom of that church. Indeed, just as the rest of the populations of the world, every Catholics will have seen God's own revelations. They will know what everyone else knows. They will see that they have an existential choice to make. These seven years of the Great Harvest will see the largest schism within the Roman church. The trickle of the exiting righteous of the last centuries will become a flood. So: The Roman Catholics everywhere will have the same opportunity as all the other people. They will be able to choose the true gospel or the non-sensical, all-inclusive and depraved gospel sold by their current leader.

The seven+ years following the Gog and Magog war will be a spiritual battlefield. Yet, amid cunning and sophisticated deceptions the world will see the largest ever harvest of souls for Jesus—the true Jesus. Incidentally, it will be a very happy time for Jesus, the Master of the harvest.

This will be the time of the great harvest: it is the time when the tares (weeds) are identified and separated from the good grain (Matthew 13:30). This is the time of the fateful polarization of mankind: the true versus the false. There will be no more delay because the good crop is ripe. How will the plants be identified as good or bad? Very simply: those who surrender and follow the true Jesus—and Him only—versus those who choose the fake messiah, the false Jesus—these are basically those who choose to follow their rebellious fancy.

The choice has to be reduced to the essentials. All the spiritual noise and distractions of today will have been eliminated by the divine events that directly precede these years (God clearly revealing Himself in actions, Gog and Magog eliminating the false gods, philosophies, etc.). When the last good plant is identified and harvested, the Great Harvest will be finished. The rest of the plants will all be deemed to be weeds and ready for the ordeal that awaits them. They are pushed aside into the testing time (Tribulations); while the good crop, just as promised, is carried with great joy and anticipation into the Master's barn (Rapture).

God allotted about seven years for this Great Harvest (it runs parallel to the incompressible seven years Ezekiel promises the Hebrews in Israel after Gog and Magog). How much more than seven years? I do not know, no one knows. But I doubt it will be long. The end of that wonderful time is signaled by the last person who having chosen the biblical Gospel of the true Messiah-Jesus will fly through the ineffective gates of Hell into the waiting arms of Jesus. At that point, there will be no one left that would readily be saved. The good harvest will be all in. Time for the good crop to celebrate in heaven.

So, Jesus will simply pick up His faithful team and leave the field—rapture. The others will experience the fate promised the tares in Matthew 13.

So, at the rapture, the other Gentile humanity will stay behind to face what is coming. The Roman Catholic Church will control an incredible number of souls. It will be perfectly positioned to carry out its long-predicted agenda of destruction that Revelation chapter 17 outlines for us. We have been amply warned.

The antichrist will have an easy task imposing his rule because all the Gentiles left then will have either refused Jesus or will have been deflected against the true Jesus; so, by definition, they will be "for" the "Jesus substitute"—the antichrist. And, they will gladly grant him instant control of their world and lives: He will seem to validate their choice. The Catholic Church will already have everybody accounted for, controlled and convinced. The antichrist will not need to win over anyone, there will not be any pitched battle to establish his reign. A few individuals will belatedly rue their choice and turn down the mark of the beast and they will be decapitated for it. But that is not organized opposition; just a mopping up operation. Jesus picks up every one of these headless saints; it is the gleaning that follows the actual harvest.

The Roman Catholic Church will be the enforcer of the antichrist's measures. It will be the beheading agent for every soul who, in extremis, says no to the mark of the beast. This evil, false Christian religion is well trained for this task because it has killed millions of true followers of Jesus over the centuries. It has shown no pity whatsoever to anyone who opposed Rome—or exposed Rome. It will show no pity to those who turn down its revealed master, Satan and his reflection, the antichrist. Poetically, the antichrist and his forces will destroy this evil church in the end.

...And this is how humanity will segue into that dreadful rule of the antichrist with his "whore"—the Roman Catholic Church—as predicted. Hopefully, many sincere Catholics of today will rethink their beliefs and allegiance during the seven+ years—post Gog and Magog and pre rapture—and leave their doomed religion. This is what Catholics have done along the centuries when they have surrendered to the true Jesus and Him only.

Notice an interesting item: In order the make the claim that the Roman Catholic Church is the only true Christian Church, Satan had to allow the Christian scriptures to exist within it—albeit buried and de-emphasized. Yet this provision proved to be the very Achilles' heel of that organization. Enough of the truth still survives in the Catholic bibles for any sincere Catholic who truly seeks Jesus to find Him there. This has been the springboard of salvation for countless Catholics over the centuries (myself included). In the scriptures we have found the good news and escaped to the Savior. The gates of Hell cannot prevail against the confession of faith to the true Jesus. Millions have been hounded to death—horrible deaths—for having escaped the Roman trap. This is also why the Catholic Church discourages personal reading of the Bible (it used to outlaw it), and why it opposes unsupervised bible studies... I am not talking about a medieval phenomenon; it is still the practice we actually faced in our twenty-first century, in a Western European country.

Sit-Rep on America

In America, will we be shielded from the power and effect of the Roman Catholic Church during the great harvest of the post Gog and Magog era? I doubt that we will.

Indeed, Americans are incredibly compromised and defenseless to the Catholic agenda. Consider how well prepared—and entrenched—the Church of Rome is for her final outreach against the people of this country:

- The majority of our Supreme Court Justices are Roman Catholics! So, the highest court of the land belongs to the enemy of the country and of its Christians members. Sobering!

- Many of our lesser judges are Roman Catholics—federal, state or local judges.

- A large percentage of our representatives and senators are Roman Catholics. Not just in Washington DC; but also in every state and organs of power. Scary!

- A very significant percentage of our military brass is Roman Catholic. Unsettling! How many member of our police forces are Catholics?

- A countless number of administrative positions, federal, state and local, are occupied by Roman Catholics. We are surrounded!

- Today (2023), we are experiencing what it is like to be ruled by a Roman Catholic president: total corruption and total evil.

- For years, we have experienced what it was like to be represented by Roman Catholic House Majority Leaders, from O'Neill to Pelosi: Total corruption and pure evil.

- We have experienced what it is like to be let down time and again by the minority opposition representation, populated by a significant ratio of Roman Catholics. We have been betrayed again and again.

When push comes to shove, history demonstrates that most Catholic will bend under Rome and will do the prelates' bidding. They always have and always will; they have to: Rome holds their ticket to Heaven. Do you see the picture?

However, during the years that follow the destruction of the fourth empire, the Roman Catholic Church will not be the supra-national power because the stone-not-cut-by-human-hands who destroys the One-World-Government / New-World-Order will grow to fill the whole earth and so; Jesus-the-stone will be the overall power through His Spirit. Just like in Jesus' parable of the wheat and the tares: the Master remains the owner of the field. The enemy who planted the tares never gets ownership of the good crop; and never controls the field operations.

So, will the Roman Catholic Church throw its weight around? Will it rig the judicial system and use its clout in the courts to punish the true Christians? Will it use the thuggish power of the Catholics in the military and police to enforce its punishments? In short: Are we going to see, in this country, the continuation of the last six hundred years of the massively deadly Inquisition? May be...

... But may be not; because these coming years will be different; they will be the special and intense time of God's rejoicing. This is divinely scheduled, divinely promised and it is outlined in the scripture: nothing will prevent it. It will be the time of the bountiful universal harvest. Traditionally, harvest is a time of celebration, of rejoicing: God who gives the harvest will be celebrating.

The Catholic Church will certainly act as desperately as it must; but Jesus, through His Spirit may simply neutralize all the Roman Catholic Church's preparations this side of the rapture. God often renders the plans of the enemy null and void, until the time comes to carry them out. Millions and millions of sincere Catholics of all walks of life who will have seen the true Jesus may listen to His gospel, and they may leave their Roman religion at that time; thus preventing the carefully planned strategy of the Catholic Church from playing out. The exit of Judges, military brass, policemen, politicians from the Roman Church toward the true and only Savior may seriously hinder the enforcing powers of the rest.

The seven+ years that follow exodus 2 and Gog and Magog could be a time of incredible blessings from above for the followers of Jesus. The One in ultimate control will still be the stone-not-cut-by-human-hand. His mediating power will be supremely efficacious. These years will be extremely frustrating for the false church and its advocates: the exuberant rejoicing all around them will be maddening to them. We can expect that this false church and its devoted adherents will play the victims as they are always wont to do. They will try to use false guilt to dull our joy and celebrations. We should never fall for any of it: our wonderful LORD will be celebrating and so should we, without reservations or any other considerations. It would be an affront to our God not to do so.

This beautiful hiatus of seven+ years—pre-rapture—will still be very different from what will take place right after it when God pulls back His mediating hand and abandons mankind to its chosen fate in what is commonly referred to as the great tribulations (or as Jesus calls it: the time of testing [Revelation 3:10]): at that time...*If anyone is to go into captivity, into captivity they will go. If anyone is to be killed with the sword, with the sword they will be killed* (Revelation 13:10). At that time, God does not interfere in the affairs of man then. (Please read the awful consequences in *Revelation the Fair God*.)

Yes, this seven+ years hiatus we are quickly approaching will be the greatest opportunity the world has ever had to harvest the Good News; but we must be vigilantly aware that the "tares" will still be around. Clean up your faith, true your doctrine, submit your will only to Him who died for you. And know what you believe... don't waver and fall into the trap of the mirror.

Conclusion

The above exercise forms a theory from which I now must coordinate all the threads to formulate how I must live, how I may control my reactions to the evolving world around me: it is the application of the scriptures. It must influence how I do things.

The following synthesis basically forms "my" conclusion: which is the implications of the scriptures for my life. And as I pondered the implications, I realized that this could become the actual conclusion of this entire piece. These are my own thoughts, so read critically in order to come to your own conclusions.

I watch what happens around me, around the parts of the world I am familiar with, I look at the prototypes of the old testament and weigh in the context of the new testament with the schedule of promises in both. On a personal level, this is what evolved in my mind.

The prototype from the Old Covenant

A prototype, a pre-production model, is usually limited in scope; and so it was with the old covenant: it was Hebraic. A prototype is also limited in time; and so it was with the old testament. The production model, being the concrete accomplishment of the prototype, is permanent and so it has been: Jesus accomplished all that the prototype was meant to accomplish and moved us into the permanent alliance of God and with God.

The prototype in antiquity had very defined successive steps:

- Moses and Aaron presented YHWH to the Hebrews.

- Moses performed the specific miracles God had told him to do for the purpose of convincing the Hebrews that Moses was legitimate and that YHWH was the true God (Exodus 4). We know what some of these miracles were.

• The Hebrews saw, they believed, and they praised YHWH (Exodus 4:31).

• Moses and Aaron told the Hebrews clearly that they would be taken out of Egypt and into their promise land by God.

• Then, Moses threw a rock in Pharaoh's pond: "Let my people go worship YHWH."

• Pharaoh, in reaction, tightened the screws on the Hebrews. He did not want his slaves to think for themselves or to act for themselves.

• The Hebrews then got the opportunity to see the Egyptian system for what it was:

- Anti YHWH,

- Overbearing,

- Not interested in their well-being,

- Vindictive,

- Unfair,

- Inane.

• And, alas, the process showed that the Hebrews feared Pharaoh more than God!

• So, they wilted and turned away from God's plan.

- And, cowardly, they turned against Moses and blamed him instead of blaming the oppressor.

- Then, God gave another set of successive miracles for Moses to perform in order to pressure Pharaoh to let God's people go—a set of plagues.

- God allowed the first three plagues to afflict the Hebrews as well as the Egyptians. God was showing the Hebrews that He was the One they should fear—not Pharaoh. The effects of the first three plagues were reversible; the losses were not permanent. God made the Hebrews experience the power God has to afflict those who don't believe.

- Then, once the Hebrews were notified of this cosmic reality; God afflicted His enemies with the rest of the plagues—terrible plagues with irreversible factors built into them.

God destroyed Egypt and its power.

What seems most significant for us today is that there were only two classes of people in that prototype: God's Hebrews and the Egyptians. There were no independent, free agents. By this, I mean that there were no Egyptians who may have humanly opposed Pharaoh's policies. These people were irrelevant. I had not seen this implication early on.

Indeed, it is conceivable that there was a part of the Egyptian population that did not agree with Pharaoh, his politics and his treatment of the Hebrew slave population. It would seem inevitable that once the entire Egyptian population began to really suffer because of Pharaoh's politics—i.e. plagues 4, 5, 6...—a body of dissenters and resisters formed and possibly even reacted.

In my mind, there is no way any population that loses their farm animals as the direct consequence of their leader's politics would not at least resent Pharaoh and most likely oppose him—whether privately, silently or vocally and overtly. In any case, God could see their hearts and minds; so why did He not differentiate among the Egyptians? Why did He smite them all the same way? A short time after the farm animals plague, there is no way an entire population and its chattel could suffer those terrible boils without reacting against the cause of their pains: Pharaoh's politics. Moses' successive meetings with Pharaoh were very public, they did not happen in secret. Moses demands and the predicted tolls he warned Pharaoh about, were made publicly and became public knowledge. Wouldn't a rebellion or at least a bitter resentment build up with each succeeding plague? The Egyptian population must have been divided.

In my opinion, the bible does not bring up the aspect of an Egyptian opposition—or at least discontentment—because it was not the central point of the story. God who saw the mind and heart of everyone did not spare the dissenters/opposers; they were lumped with their regime. And, on the night of the departure, the ones who thought well of the Hebrews and who gave them riches to take away had not been spared by God. They had had horrible losses, they were financially gutted and they were mourning their first borns just like the rest of the Egyptians loyal to Pharaoh.

It struck me that through the entire process, God considered only two classes of people: His people and Pharaoh's people. For God's purpose, there were not three groups there—that is: 1) The Hebrews, 2) the "good Egyptians" and 3) Pharaoh's loyalists. So, today, wouldn't there be only two people also in our countries where exodus 2.0 will begin?... And not three as in: 10 God's people, then 2) the "good Americans" and finally 3) the evil Deep State of the fourth empire?

So then, let's look at today.

The new covenant, Today's parallels and equivalents

The new covenant is universal. It is the "production model". It is permanent. In our time, the scope of exodus 2.0 is not limited to one country. It brings out the fulness of God's plan. The parallel of the historical process runs as follows:

• Beginning at the dawn of our era with the Jews in Israel, Messiah Jesus and the new life were presented to us all. The new alliance is universal (not just Hebraic like Moses' was). The written record of it all is available to all: we can all know Jesus/YHWH.

• To convince all of His identity and mission, Jesus did many miracles—well recorded miracles—culminating with His divine resurrection.

• Many people then and since have believed and praised Him over the years and centuries.

• The fourth empire has targeted Jesus' follower relentlessly since its inception.

• Recently, leaders like Trump, Bolsonaro, Orban and Putin threw a rock in the Globalists' One-World-Government pond. "Let the people go!"

• In response, the Deep State mercilessly ratcheted their controls and constraints. The onslaught is daily; from petty controls to universal fears to spiritual tyranny. It parallels Pharaoh's actions in the prototype.

• Now we are at the brink of exodus 2.0.

• Predictably, in an attempt to placate the tyrants, some of Jesus' followers turn against the rock throwers—just as the Hebrews did against Moses and Aaron.

• Today's populations, especially those who follow Jesus can see how:

- Anti Jesus,

- Overbearing,

- Intrusive,

- Uncaring,

- Vindictive,

- Senseless,

- Unfair and

- Murderous the Globalists' One-World-Government's Deep State is.

I think we are in this discovery phase. So, who will I look up to? And whom will I fear?

• Jesus will destroy our "Egyptian type" state and power: The Globalists' One-World-Government.

• But, I, as follower of Jesus, where am I in my faith? Do I fear the Globalists' One-World-Government more than I trust the promises God made to me as a believer? (Such promises are legion in the Bible; see one at random: Nahum 1:5 – 7.)

• The cowardly churches' response to the COVID mandates madness mimicked the Hebrew leaders reaction to Pharaoh's repression and it has crumpled the hypocritical facade of organized religion.

• Will we still need to be reminded whom to fear?... Will we too need to go through some of God's coming plagues? Shame on us if we have to. Shame on me if I don't pro-act.

• The Globalists' One-World-Government and its Deep State are ratcheting the pressure. They are taking away our freedoms, our voice, opposing our abilities, denying our identities. So, do I fear them more than the righteous God who will act soon? The very Rock that will destroy that empire? It is time I leave philosophy and live the faith.

Other considerations assailed me. Was Moses' premature attempt to free his people, on his own strength, forty years earlier, an equivalent of Trump, Bolsonaro and Putin's attempts at fighting the fourth empire? Back then, Moses was taken away for a long stretch. Do we have to wait for a long stretch today? No, I don't think so, because we are already into the hardening phase of the reactionary "Egyptian type" abuse.

Other consideration: Do we need a modern day Moses? I don't know. Moses fulfilled two functions: He led his people out of Egypt of course, but lastingly he provided them (and us all) with the Law, the Pentateuch. Today, and for a long while already, the knowledge of God/Jesus has been readily available to His people universally. In Moses' time, this knowledge had not been recorded yet. It was not accessible. A leader like Moses was needed as a lawgiver. We don't need a "lawgiver"; we already have all the information.

So, I think that God is getting ready to act.

There are other differences: today a significant number of believers in every country are pushing back against the fourth empire's severe and cavalier encroachment. These awakened folks can see through the mandates and past the censure; these believers fear God more than the State.

This small but enduring faction who look to God as the solution and the power over all is a significant element in today's situation. Are they the collective "Moses and Aaron" of today?

Just like in Moses's time, these small pockets of populations are also vilified by the "sheeple among them" who would rather appease our ogreish Pharaoh through demeaning kowtowing. When we stand like Moses, we make the "sheeples" afraid of the Pharaonic reactions, and our own people, friends, family may turn against us.

When I read or listen to bellicose arguments against the Deep State, I am reminded that while Moses and Aaron were used as God's intermediaries between Himself and Satan's Pharaonic minion, Moses and Aaron did not fight. They did not carry out God's actions. The actions remained 100% divine. Moses did not get credit for any of them—nor was he held responsible for any of them. Pharaoh could see clearly the hand of God behind Moses' warnings and thence came Moses' protection.

And Moses never bent, never retracted, never retreated and never apologized. He kept his stark divine messages in Pharaoh's face.

Unlike in his doomed attempt forty years earlier when he killed a bellicose Egyptian, Moses did not carry a sword, he never individually struck a person with sickness, he never killed chattel with hail... Moses did not kill a single one of the first born Egyptians. God did, and everyone knew that God did.

So, how does all this harmonize for me with the upcoming exodus 2.0 and the destruction of the fourth empire? Will each of God's strikes destroys an aspect, a dimension of the fourth empire?

A reality I had ignored began to establish itself: I have been looking at America from the wrong perspective. I have seen America as a population of "mostly good guys" who just need cleaning up. But, the fourth empire <u>is</u> America, just as the fourth empire <u>is</u> England and <u>is</u> Israel… The fourth empire is not just "a part" of America; it is America.

The two kind of people inhabiting every country of the fourth empire are: God's people, (the Hebrews and the followers of Jesus), and the fourth empire. In God's perspective, there was no third group in Egypt, and as I see it now, this reality applies universally to every country today: there are no third groups. The reason there are only two groups is that the situation is spiritual—not political—and spiritually, there are only two kinds of people: God's people and all the others.

Pharaoh's rule was Egypt; his rule was not just an element of Egypt. Pharaoh's rule and Egypt were one entity in God's eyes. Today, the fourth empire is America, it is England, it is Israel, and every other country; it is not a faction of the population of these countries—it is not an aspect of their administrations. So, in America, we only have the fourth kingdom and the true followers of Jesus.

To repeat, we are now at a time when the choices are not political anymore; they are spiritual: To be set apart in Jesus or to be a part of the edifice that the Stone will break. Our time is a time of decisions, the owner is coming to straighten things out. And it is a time when our actions should match and reflect our convictions. It is a time like never before. It makes sense that the only consideration would be Jesus or not Jesus; because this short period of Jesus' destructive actions will segue directly into the what I call the greatest harvest of all times (During the seven years+ that God rejoices with the full harvest of the Hebrews in

Israel). A while ago, unaware, we have stepped into a time when politics is not where the game is.

I had made the mistake of following the wishful arguments of the various groups of conservatives—some true disciples of Jesus, others not—who want to rally and storm the barricades of the Deep State. This perspective gave me the impression that there was a viable mixed population opposed to the Deep State. A workable coalition made of Christians and non-Christians standing against the overt evil that faces us. A civic majority that could weigh in and win, thus effecting the needed changes.

I was wrong. I now see only two groups: God's followers and the fourth empire. I still struggle with this reality because I don't like it. I had embraced the "good Americans" faction because the politics of our fourth empire's Pharaohs are so totally offensive that they don't represent most people I know and love. (And also because I love my country.) Now I see that the stakes are far more stark.

So, I will stop following the mythical third group who bandies a human resistance based only on integrity and conservative philosophical points of view. In the end, they are not where the action will be. They are not the solution.

I see that, right on clue, the Deep State is feverishly pushing its "Great Reset", the universal fulcrum over which they hope their total takeover will irreversibly tip. The reality is clear: Satan is desperately trying to outrun God's plan and prevent what is really coming. Based on history, it is expected that he would endeavor to do so. And, also based on history: he will fail, but his push will have killed many and destroyed the lives of millions more. I now realize that mobilizing against the "Great Reset" is a fool's trap. I have wasted my angst, hopes and energies on a reality that will soon be moot.

Yes, I will resist, I will say no, I will not accept any of the non-Christlike edicts and mandates. I will speak the biblical truth and I will not hold back. But I will not be active in taking the Deep State down, in destroying it. I don't need to and should not even consider it; God took on that job a long time ago. I will give Him a wide berth.

No matter what edict the Deep State enacts, it will soon have no teeth at all. Let's consider the Hebrews in Egypt; when the conditions of their miserable lives were made worse, they could not have overturned the Pharaonic system by banding together and gone on the offensive. Pharaoh had all the weapons and all the human might.

Yet, on the other hand, had they acted on their new found faith in their God; they could have said no to the conditions imposed on them. Especially when we consider that from the time the first plague hit, the Egyptians were not able to enforce any of their repressive measures! It was over! The tyranny died with the first plague. The Hebrews could have said: "No, we will not make bricks plus find the necessary straw for the making of the bricks. We believe our God is with us." What would have happened? Their turncoat taskmasters might have been severely beaten before the first plague hit; but certainly, the Egyptians could not have systematically gone around and beaten every Hebrew to a pulp. That was not possible. And it would have defeated the Egyptians' purpose.

The Hebrews simply failed to trust God and thus fell to a fear that by then was all but irrational. They would not consider a perspective outside their past understanding; they would not apply their newfound faith.

It is the same here and now. Can the power-that-be actually come down on every believer who says no? And if the cabal began to do this; could they finish it? The realistic answer to both questions is no. The Cabal's time is extremely limited. And, once God begins His process, the Cabal's fangs are instantly knocked off. The Rock's first strike will disarm the fourth empire. If I belong to Jesus, fearing the power of the Deep State today is shortsighted, and like in Egypt; it is irrational. Yes, some of us may suffer...for a time; but again, we may not! We are His children whom He loves and in whom He is well pleased.

I am not burying my head in the sand; on the contrary, having faced the facts head-on and drawn what I see as the proper course, I can now stand firm in my convictions and rest on my hope. I will simply leave the maddening vortex of human tit-for-tats, the breathless jockeying-for-advantage that can draw the helpless and hapless observer down a funnel of doom. I will look up and see what the God of the universe is doing and what He will do. From my protected "Goshen" I will watch and praise the divine events happening in today's "Global Egypt".

Back then for exodus 1.0, in old Egypt, the political and military power was completely destroyed. For exodus 2.0, I expect that the punitive political and military powers of every country where the followers of Jesus and the Hebrews live, will be completely destroyed.

In Egypt, an impoverished and mourning percentage of the Egyptian population was left alive (the head of state and his instrument of power were killed—an ominous reality). While God's people left with the loot. At exodus 2.0, we can expect that a large percentage of the non-followers of Jesus will survive, impoverished and mourning—but they will be left alive. The followers of Jesus and the Hebrews will get the loot.

My beloved America may still be called America because that's what the maps say; but it will be irrelevant as a global power—just as Egypt became irrelevant as a power for quite a stretch of time. And so it will be for all the countries that the fourth empire controls. Daniel 2 makes this point clearly: the Stone that destroys the fourth empire will remain and grow to fill the entire earth: No human state-power will ever again project its might as we have done.

However, cleansed of the nefarious fourth empire, America could be a vibrant and striving country. Especially during the exuberant Great Harvest that will follow shortly after—a time of joyous celebration. I think we are headed for a far better time than we can imagine. We have millions of true followers of Jesus who will explode with joy!

One more item regarding the absence of the United States of America on the side of Israel during the war of Gog and Magog: It is vital to remember that our warmongers will be dead; they are all stooges of the Deep State—the fourth empire. Their murderous whipping up of the public opinion will never happen again. American true followers of Jesus will see clearly and they will calm the public opinion. We will understand what is truly happening at Gog and Magog. At any rate, the war will be so short; it will be over before any foreign involvement could have an effect anyway.

As for me, I know God placed me in my beloved country, at this specific time to be one of the stalwart stitches of redeemed living in the fabric of this country. This being the case, the fabric cannot completely unravel as long as that stitch holds... And there are thousands of such stitches across our land, old and young, men and women... The fabric will not rip as long as these individual stitches hold. Being aware of this; I know my personal responsibility. I will carry out, moment by moment, the small tasks God gives me. I will not being tossed about by the politico-social events at large. I am aware of these events, yet I understand and know their true meaning and their ultimate fate. God wrote the script long ago.

So, for me, the message of God to Baruch (Jeremiah 45) becomes very relevant: *I will overthrow what I have built and uproot what I have planted, <u>through out the earth</u>. Should you then seek great things* *for yourself? Do not seek them. For I will bring a disaster <u>on all people</u>, declares the LORD, but wherever you go I will let you escape with your life [or: grant you your life like the spoils/plunder of war]* (Emphasis is mine).

Keeping up with the suspenseful back-and-forth skirmishes between the resisters and the Deep State has kept me on pins and needles. I need to relax: their activities may end up being just a side show, a non-event for us believers. The fixing will be God's; not the "patriots'". I must stop worrying about how this or how new development will affect me. It is not the reality I should embrace. Indeed, there are two humanities out there: Jesus' flock and all the other people. Those in Jesus' flock will be firmly in His grip and taken care of by Him, the Shepherd; no matter what is happening outside.

Recently I had a sort of epiphany: as a believer, I realized that I don't need the elite—neither the elite of the progressive left, nor the elite of the not-so-conservative right; they are parasites. They produce nothing and they can do nothing for me.

What are humans yearning for? We all yearn for security and for satisfied needs. For the last two and a-half centuries, the fourth empire has demonstrated that they do not provide security. Indeed, they have consistently plotted, fomented and financed wars.

As far as providing for the people's needs, no socialist style of government has ever provided for the needs of its sheeples. They have engineered famines everywhere, ruined the medicine of healing and created epidemics. Their "relief" agencies are mired in corruption and never accomplish any progress at all. And don't forget, they want us to eat bugs and to switch to factory engineered and manufactured foodstuff...

But the good news is that for the follower of Jesus, security is shouldered by the One, the true, and only God. I have His commitment to be my actual fortress, my defender, my shepherd around trouble (Psalm 46:1 – 3, 27:5, 31:20, 91:2, Deuteronomy 33:27, and many more passages). So, for security and survival: I don't need the elite. (I don't even need a victorious conservative right.)

Now regarding food, drink, or status (as well as all other human needs), Jesus my Lord has taken on these tasks. He prepares a meal in the presence of my enemies (Psalm 23:5), He knows all my needs and will provide them (Matthew 6:25 – 33). If I am true to my faith, my living does not depend on anything these government flunkies claim to offer!

Away from persnickety old England, our forefathers, realized that in the new land, their safety and security and the fulfillment of their needs depended on the Creator and not on the ineffectual crowd of Crown flunkies on their distant island. This basis gave them the impetus to dream of a better government. Having the divine perspective, they foresaw a free people in control of a small government—a service government; a government in their service. They also predicted that if the people cast away the divine anchor of their lives; the glorious experiment would quickly fail and tyranny would reassert itself—which it did and which it has. So, today's America is the proof that the issue was and will always be spiritual.

...So, I have no need for what the obnoxious, invasive apparatus people purport to have; but, on the other hand, they need what I have. They need the good news about the life and the life more abundantly—the life of the free. This is not about Heaven or Hell; it is about life here and now. They are parasites with empty promises. I have what they need; they are the needy ones. Being clear that I don't need them has freed me from the tug of war in my heart that the war of information from both side had stoked in me.

The psalmist says: *The LORD is my shepherd, I will always have everything I need. Even though I walk through the valley of deep darkness,*

I fear no harm; for you are with me. Your rod and your staff, they comfort me. You do prepare a table before me in the presence of my enemies; you do anoint my head with oil: My cup overflows... (Psalm 23). Time has not eroded this principle. Isaiah 8 tells us: *The LORD spoke to me with his great power and warned me not to be like these people. He said: Don't think there is a plan against you just because people say there is... Don't let them frighten you. The LORD All-Powerful is the one you should fear... If you people would respect him, he should be a safe place for you.* So, yes, the enemy threatens us at all levels; but can he outwit, out-power the Shepherd? No, he cannot. No matter what the fourth empire threatens to do to us all; let someone else worry about it. As for you, bask in your position in His flock; you will always eat, always rest, always be cared for. Whatever the evil actors plan to do to us; they must first get by the Shepherd... Good luck with that!

When God's kingdom was begun by Jesus, the Hebrews/Jews, led, bullied and prodded by the small cabal of the Pharisees rejected Jesus' kingdom. They were the first tyrants to fight relentlessly against it. In Acts, we read that the Jewish minority even had the cheek to whip up foreign societies against the good news and demand its presenters' death—they overreached well outside their own country of Judea... so great was their hatred. This Pharisaic cabal has not changed. It was already the worldwide anti-Jesus agent of antiquity, and has remained so. Their Talmudic heresy continued to harden since then. This Talmudic heresy will be crushed by Jesus through His process of vetting Jacob's descendants for exodus 2.0.

The fourth empire—that seems to be a kind of extension of the Pharisaic/Talmudic hatred of Jesus—has a very, very vast military-industrial complex. The might it can wield is terrifying. It is vicious, pitiless and immensely proud. But it is human; not divine—just like Pharaoh's might was.

As we have proposed through this essay: the very Divine Factor these people have aimed to destroy since antiquity is the very Divine Factor that will destroy them finally. The Rock will soon destroy the historical projection of the nefarious Pharisaic cabal who, all along, opposed Him and His kingdom. And thus held God's ancient people in spiritual bondage.

Rid of this evil minority, the descendants of Jacob will go on from blessings to blessings and the rest of humanity will have a righteous choice to make: the Rock on one hand or the pretender on the other. We are on the threshold of God's march of glory.

The Globalists One-World-Government/New-World-Order is as good as dead—in our time; before the "tribulations". We can bank on God for it and thank Him!

This is my conclusions; what will yours be?

Postscript

Ebooks and print on demand offer the author the invaluable ability to provide living documents. As events unfold, as dates roll by, the text can easily be updated to bring into focus facets dimly seen that have become readily apparent. I intend to carry out this running update. This ebook is offered without charge on most platforms so that—should you choose to—you may access the latest updated text anytime you want. Print on demand books will be priced at cost—that is to say without royalties.

Thank you,

Pierre-Louis Ours

www.ingramcontent.com/pod-product-compliance
Lightning Source LLC
Chambersburg PA
CBHW021437150726
47989CB00001B/273